D1472425

Other books by Jeffry H. Larson

Should We Stay Together?

Effective Stepparenting

The Great
Marriage
Tune-Up Book

The Great Marriage Tune-Up Book

A PROVEN PROGRAM FOR
EVALUATING AND RENEWING
YOUR RELATIONSHIP

Jeffry H. Larson, Ph.D.

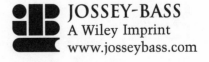

JOSSEY-BASS
A Wiley Imprint
www.josseybass.com

Published by Jossey-Bass
A Wiley Imprint
989 Market Street, San Francisco, CA 94103-1741   www.josseybass.com

Jossey-Bass is a registered trademark of John Wiley & Sons, Inc.

Jossey-Bass books and products are available through most bookstores. To contact Jossey-Bass
directly, call (888) 378-2537, fax to (800) 605-2665, or visit our website at www.josseybass.com.

Substantial discounts on bulk quantities of Jossey-Bass books are available to corporations, professional associations, and other organizations. For details and discount information, contact the
special sales department at Jossey-Bass.

We at Jossey-Bass strive to use the most environmentally sensitive paper stocks available to us. Our publications are printed on acid-free recycled stock whenever possible, and our paper always meets or
exceeds minimum GPO and EPA requirements.

Jossey-Bass also publishes its books in a variety of electronic formats. Some content that appears in print
may not be available in electronic books.

Library of Congress Cataloging-in-Publication Data

Larson, Jeffry H.
   The great marriage tune-up book: a proven program for evaluating and renewing your relationship /
Jeffry H. Larson.—1st ed.
      p. cm.
Includes bibliographical references.
   ISBN 0-7879-6212-0 (alk. paper)
   1. Marriage. 2. Marriage counseling. I. Title.
   HQ734 .L3354 2002
   306.81—dc21
2002006582
FIRST EDITION
PB Printing   10 9 8 7 6 5 4 3 2 1

Contents

Acknowledgments

Several people deserve my sincere thanks for helping with this project. Thanks to Alan Rinzler, executive editor at Jossey-Bass, for his encouragement and support throughout the conceptualization, organization, and editing of this book. Special thanks to Dr. Tom Holman and my associates at the RELATE Institute for giving me permission to use questions from the RELATionship Evaluation questionnaire. My association with this group has been one of the highlights of my academic career. Thanks also to Jennifer Reynolds and Suzanne Huffman for typing the manuscript in a timely and professional manner.

Finally, I express my love and gratitude to my wife, Jeannie, and my children for putting up with me and my long work hours while I wrote this book. My greatest wish is that my family and friends will use the concepts in this book to improve their marriages!

August 2002   J.H.L.

To the many couples who want
to have more than just an average
marriage—but rather, a great marriage!

Introduction

For more than two decades I have done research into how couples stay happily married and have helped hundreds of couples do just that in marriage enrichment workshops and courses and in marital therapy. This has been very fulfilling, but I have always wondered why couples do not follow the car maintenance model in their marriages. That is, they get regular oil changes and tune-ups for their cars but never think of getting regular marriage checkups or tune-ups. This book will show you how to do a marital checkup and tune-up.

The analogy to auto maintenance makes sense: you go to your mechanic on a regular basis to have him check the vital signs of your engine, transmission, tires, and other components. At least you do this regularly if you want your car to last a long time and give you good service. The mechanic checks a number of important areas—computer functioning, engine functioning, tire wear, fluid levels, and so on—and tells you what actions need to be taken now to keep it going and to avoid bigger problems and repairs later. By frequently checking the air pressure and rotating the tires, for example, you can extend the life of the tires or at least get the full fifty thousand miles promised in the warranty. Although marriage doesn't come with a warranty and we cannot insure it for one hundred thousand miles (or a lifetime), if you maintain it regularly, you will significantly increase the chances of its still running well at one hundred thousand miles.

But did anyone give you instructions on regular marriage maintenance when you got married? I know that no one handed me a maintenance schedule. An official just told us how wonderful we were, never to argue before bedtime, and to go off and have a happy life together. Everyone just assumed it would happen. Sound familiar?

Well, it's never too late to get on track with a marriage checkup and tune-up. Considering that it's the most important relationship in your life, it's worth the effort. But where do you start? What factors predict your current and future marital satisfaction? What can fifty years of social science research tell us about the condition of your marriage and help you have the best chance for many years of happiness ahead? That's the dual focus of this book: checkup (assessment) and tune-up (enrichment).

𝕤 Purpose of This Book

More specifically, this book will do all of the following things:

1. It will answer these questions: Why, inevitably, does marriage become stale or unsatisfying if you're not careful? Is there a developmental model of the stages of marriage that can help you predict downturns and how to get through them?

2. It will explain the myths about marriage common in our culture that exacerbate the problems even more—for example, "Romantic love lasts forever" and "My spouse should meet all of my needs."

3. It will reveal the two dozen or so specific factors that predict marital satisfaction using a simple but comprehensive model called the Marriage Triangle.

4. It will provide comprehensive checkup questions based on this model to assess your own marital strengths and liabilities.

5. It will help you decide how to tune up your marriage by overcoming liabilities in yourself, your relationship, or the context or environment in which you live.

6. It will show you where to get help to tune up your marriage so that it will be not just an average marriage but a great one!

At the end of your assessments in this book, you may discover that your marriage needs only an oil change or perhaps a minor tune-up. Or you may learn that you need a major tune-up or even an overhaul. Again, the analogy between your car and your marriage makes sense. For example, usually it is less painful and less costly to fix up the usually reliable sedan you love than to trade it in for a more expensive, newer model that comes with built-in defects of its own (yes, new cars do come with multiple defects along with those higher payments!). And tune-ups and overhauls usually result in many more miles of comfortable and satisfying driving.

🎱 A Tune-Up Example

Let's look at an example of what I mean by tuning up your marriage by looking at a couple I saw in marital therapy a few years ago.

Tom (thirty-five) and Sheila (thirty-two) had been married for nine years. He worked as a computer software technician, and she was assistant manager at a women's clothing store in the local mall. They had two children, aged six and four. I suggested in our first session that they read the materials that ultimately became this book and complete the assessment questions. They answered all the questions and scored themselves and came back with the following summary report:

They both felt career-stressed. Sheila was working about fifty hours a week, and Tom was holding down two jobs—his regular job with a local computer firm and private contracts with businesses on the side. They reported financial strain, admitting that the home they had recently purchased was in fact more than they could afford. They saw no way of getting out of the high house payment. The financial strain led to frequent verbal fights with no resolution, and so the problem kept reasserting itself. Tom and Sheila were clearly tired of fighting about finances.

The couple also wanted to be great parents, and it seemed that they spent all the rest of their time parenting. In fact, they had not gone out together alone for dinner or a movie in nearly six months! They had not taken a vacation alone since their honeymoon. The picture they painted was clear: working overtime in their careers, working overtime with their children, and neglecting their marriage.

In addition, certain personal traits were aggravating the situation. Sheila reported not dealing with stress well, being anxious all the time, and being a perfectionist at work and with the children. She said she had a history of low self-esteem (often related to perfectionism) that dated from childhood and said it stemmed from growing up in a dysfunctional family.

Tom discovered as a result of completing the assessments that he was more depressed than he originally thought. He also felt overworked and underappreciated by his boss. Tom also learned from the assessments that his conflict resolution style was not as healthy as it could be. He tended simply to give up and walk away when conflict started. This approach only infuriated Sheila more, and their discussions resulted in an unhealthy pursuing-distancing style of conflict resolution.

Sheila complained that Tom was also too quiet—he never talked about his feelings much except to blow up during a conflict. He reported no role models of healthy self-disclosure in his family of origin. He described his father as a strong, silent man.

Both spouses reported dissatisfaction with their sex life, centered primarily around too infrequent relations and fatigue most of the time. This resulted in lower sexual desire on the part of both of them. But when they did have sex, they said it was usually great. Related to their lack of sexual intimacy was a lack of fun times together. It seemed that whenever they had a few hours of time available for recreation, it was always spent with the kids at amusement parks, at swimming holes, or on the ski slopes rather than doing things together alone. This problem was reflected in Sheila's statement that they never seemed to have fun together anymore.

At one point in our therapy sessions, they exclaimed, "When we got married, we loved each other and were fully committed to making this work for the long haul. But we're not having fun, and it's grinding us down. We're wondering, is this all there is? We thought that with love and commitment, the marriage would just take care of itself. It hasn't!"

Based on their assessments, we decided their marriage needed a major tune-up. Communication skills training was a major part of it. With better conflict resolution skills, they started resolving their financial problems. Tom learned how to self-disclose more. Sheila read a self-help book and did some individual counseling with me to gain a better understanding of her sources of anxiety, stress, and perfectionism. Tom worked on getting over his depression with some counseling, self-help reading, and a short course of medication.

A major attitude change that occurred in this case was when Tom and Sheila began to prioritize their marriage more—to put it first in their lives instead of last after careers, kids, and housework. As a result, they noticed a drastic change in their affection toward each other, and their sex life improved as they spent more time alone every Friday night. Both cut back on their hours at work and spent those hours instead together alone, learning how to cope with stress better, getting more exercise, exploring other career options for Tom, and planning a more realistic budget so that they weren't so "house poor."

Their tune-up took them four months to execute. If they were to answer the questions in this book again today, they would see significant improvements in all of their scores. Their success was based on three firm commitments:

1. A commitment to improving their marriage and a willingness to change

2. A commitment to learning what to assess, how to assess it, and what to do with the results (this book provided those things)

3. A commitment to changing their behavior and attitudes—resolving conflict in a healthier way, spending every Friday night alone together enjoying each other's company, resolving personal hang-ups, and employing better stress management techniques

You, too, can have the same success!

What's Next in This Book

Chapter One will describe how a marriage develops over time—especially in the early years—and normalizes many of the stresses and challenges you have found in your own marriage. The important thing to remember is that most of these issues are resolvable! In addition to explaining how marriage problems develop, I will discuss the myths about marriage and about improving marriage that combine with the daily stresses of married life to cause major problems and roadblocks to resolving problems.

Chapter Two discusses the three main factors in the marriage triangle that predict marital satisfaction and gets you started assessing your own marriage. In Chapters Three, Four, and Five, you will assess your marriage on the basis of each of these factors—individual traits like personality, couple traits like communication skills, and contexts like family backgrounds. At the end of each chapter, you will set goals for improving your marriage in each of these areas. Chapter Six is where you summarize the results of your assessments and set goals for improvement. Chapter Seven prescribes resources for improving your marriage and offers advice on how to get into therapy. Books, tapes, CDs, education programs, retreats, and how to find a therapist are described in detail.

The purpose of all of this, of course, is to help you tune up your marriage so it will become *great*—perhaps even greater than you imagined it could be.

The Great
Marriage
Tune-Up Book

Overcoming Myths About Marriage

Most couples have never participated in marriage education of any kind except what they've read in newspapers and magazines. No one told them when they married what adjustments they would need to make in the early years of marriage. Few of us know on our wedding day that our relationship will go through predictable stages as we adjust to being husband and wife. Even if you have lived together for some time, being married is cognitively, emotionally, legally, spiritually, and socially different. Our expectations of each other change when we assume the husband and wife roles. For example, one of you is now expected to manage "the" checkbook effectively. Now you expect to discuss large purchases with each other rather than making unilateral expenditure decisions as you did when you were single.

Not only do we now expect more of each other, but we fail to understand that our love for each other is going to change too, from a romantic love to a more companionate love (friendship). I call these changes the three stages of marriage. All couples experience these three stages in some form or another. Some couples go through these relationship stages faster than others. Some get stuck in one for a significant period of time. Let's look at how the problem of marital malaise gets started and solutions to not getting stuck.

❧ The Three Stages of Marriage

Most marriages develop through three stages, in this order:

1. Romantic love

2. Disillusionment and distraction

3. Dissolution or adjustment with resignation or contentment

Stage 1: Romantic Love

Most couples get married in a state of romantic love that many describe as ecstasy. *Ecstasy* comes from a Greek word meaning "deranged."[1] That is, our love at this stage in our marriage is primarily sexual, passionate, irrational, and based on physical attraction. It's all the more ecstatic because communication at this stage is relatively easy with much rapport. At this stage you have not had to make any big sacrifices; you have experienced no major crises yet. You intentionally, although somewhat unconsciously, show your partner only your good side—for example, watching your physical appearance and dress so that you continue to dazzle your partner and make him think he's the luckiest guy in the world.

Our expectations of our partner and the relationship are also irrational during this honeymoon period. We may expect our partner to meet all of our needs for acceptance and love. You may see him as the ultimate protector or her as the ultimate nurturer, your fountain of affection and caring. You finally found the person who will heal your inner wound from the past and meet all your emotional needs. Romantic love like this is mother nature's way of attracting men and women to each other long enough for a more stable and meaningful relationship to take seed and begin to grow. In this stage of marriage, couples report, "Oh, I love him so much—he's perfect for me!" "I want to make you the happiest woman in the world!" "You have made me the happiest guy in the world!" It's like whirling around in a tornado of romance. Great fun! Mother nature has done her job well! But after a while it's time to settle in to being *really* married and experiencing both the highs and the lows of married life. Couples then move into stage 2.

Stage 2: Disillusionment and Distraction

The problem with romantic love is that inevitably, sooner or later, it slips away. "The honeymoon always ends. The bloom of romance always fades."[2] As romantic love diminishes, other challenges begin to appear in our personal and couple lives. Daily life is stressful by itself. Learning to share the bathroom, working out marital roles (who cleans the toilet or takes out the garage, who initiates sex, who manages the checkbook, and so on) and the stress associated with balancing two careers and still making time for each other all take a toll on us physically and emotionally, and the vitality of our relationship suffers. These occurrences are not inherently bad—they are an unavoidable part of life. But they are more difficult transitions than we thought they would be. In addition, some of our fantasies just do not come true; for example, we are surprised and even shocked at realizations like these:

He isn't always thinking of me.

She doesn't call me every day at work to say, "I love you."

He is a bit more overweight than I originally thought. How did I miss that?

I thought she was going to work too. Now I have to make all the money, and there isn't enough.

Wow, does he have a temper when he doesn't get enough rest! Where did that come from?

In short, marriage ultimately disappoints you as well as fulfills you. This natural but painful difference between fantasy and reality (discovered months *after* the wedding) commonly leads to disillusionment.

It is also disillusioning to discover that meshing two distinct personalities is more challenging than you thought it would be. Personality traits not revealed during courtship or the honeymoon start to appear when you're under stress—anger not seen before, depression on certain days of the month, or irritability that sometimes goes on for days.

Perhaps most shocking, now your partner shows you his dark or more basic side: he "forgets" to shave while on vacation, throws his clothes on your path to the bathroom, and scratches where it itches! In other words, having won over our partner by showing her our most positive behaviors (this used to be called courtship) and then marrying her, we now relax (sometimes too much) and show her the other side. This other side does not stimulate romantic love! We're caught in a situation where we want to change our partner and may even regret marrying him. All this is normal—Marriage Adjustment 101. (Does that make you feel any better? I hope so!)

Add to these changes in the relationship and your circumstances a stressful event or a crisis (buying a home, the arrival of children and the stresses of parenting, a chronic illness, a miscarriage, loss of a valued job) and the resultant sacrifices you have to make to get along with your partner, and it's enough to send many couples into a tailspin. An example of this occurred with Ron and Barbara. After three years of marriage, they were still wading through the disillusionment phase. Each struggled to adjust to the other's idiosyncrasies. Ron would often "hole up" in the den and play computer games after dinner; that upset Barbara, who expected him to sit on the porch with her and talk about the ups and downs of the day. They struggled to find a balance between private time and couple time. In the midst of trying to compromise on these different needs, they decided to build a home with a contractor. This process, filled with countless decisions, planning, financial hassles, late-night conversations, paperwork, disappointments, and frustrations, added tremendous stress to a marriage that was already in the disillusionment phase. The stress resulted in more frequent arguments, irritability, and fatigue. As a wise friend once told me, "Any marriage that can survive building a house is a very strong marriage!" The house-building stress combined with the unresolved issue of togetherness versus separateness almost sank Ron and Barbara's marriage entirely.

Life also holds out many natural distractions that cause us to focus away from our marriage and onto other life necessities, such as raising children; working and paying the bills; advancing in our careers; engaging in hobbies, sports, recreation, television, or the Internet; and PTA or other community meetings. None of these distractions are inherently harmful—they just rob us of time together as a couple, unless we can arrange to do some of them together (hobbies, sports, children). We become too busy for our marriages. And dating activities as a couple cease entirely, especially after children have come into the picture.

This combination of disillusionment and distraction also hurts your sex life. Two of the most common causes of sexual problems in marriage—stress and fatigue—are the result of many of the distractions I listed. We become "spread too thin" emotionally and physically, leaving too little time and energy for our relationship, let alone for our sex life. And sexual boredom may occur as a result of not being more creative and playful in our private moments.

Now some good news! Most couples make it past this stage and end up with a vital, satisfying marriage. You can, too. Let's look at what happens in the next stage to determine where you will eventually settle.

Stage 3: Dissolution or Adjustment with Resignation or Contentment

By the time couples get to the end of stage 2, they know there is something wrong with their marriage. Feeling disappointed and discontent, the question is, "What should we do?" You have three options.

1. You can give up, *dissolving the relationship* through separation or divorce.

2. You can just keep on trying to survive, day to day, in an unsatisfying marriage—I call this *adjusting with resignation*. There is little love in such a marriage. Couples in resigned marriages grow progressively apart, and their lives end up on parallel tracks, much like living with a roommate who has her own life and rarely shares it with you. They stay together because they are afraid or feel too guilty to divorce, fear the effects of divorce on their children, or cannot afford to split. They lead lives of marital mediocrity and think there are no good solutions out there for them except to keep plodding along.

3. You can decide to be more content. *Adjusting with contentment* occurs when you still love each other, but your love has become more like a good friendship with some passion thrown in. Altruistic love may have developed by now too. This is the self-giving kind of love that is kind and patient, not demanding. It's the kind of love defined by Harry Stack Sullivan, a famous psychiatrist, as "when the satisfaction or the security of another person becomes as significant as is one's own satisfaction or security."[3] I'm suggesting that a successful marriage is based on all three types of love: romantic, companionate, and altruistic. Adjusting with contentment also requires an awareness of your marital situation and the areas you want to improve in your relationship to become more content. Then add commitment to improving your marriage and the tools with which to do it. With some dedicated work and adjustments, your marriage will improve. The purpose of this book is to help you begin this process, which will ultimately result in greater contentment.

❧ It's Your Decision

So where is your marriage right now? Probably in stage 2 or 3, or you wouldn't be reading this book. What do you want to do? Unfortunately, too many couples choose alternative 1 or 2. Everyone knows that the divorce rate in the United States is too high. But few people acknowledge that the number of unhappy but stable (unseparated or undivorced) couples in the country is nearly as high as the divorce rate (currently, about 40 percent of couples who marry will eventually divorce). What a shame, to live your married life in resigned misery or mediocrity. It's a national health problem.

But you do not have to be in either of these groups. Instead, you can choose to be in group 3. Let's look at what couples need to do to be in group 3.

First, there has to be an acknowledgment by both spouses that their marriage needs a thoughtful checkup or assessment and perhaps a tune-up. Second, you need an increased awareness of the strengths and weaknesses of each of you as individuals and of the relationship itself. Third, you need an awareness of factors in the context or environment of your marriage that hurt the marriage—for example, overwork, overparenting, or stressors not coped with adequately enough to protect the vitality of the marriage. Fourth, you need a plan for improving individual traits (such as emotional health) and couple traits (such as conflict resolution skills) and for improving your ability to deal more effectively with stressors, parenting, careers, and other factors that may negatively affect your marriage. Fifth and finally, you need to commit wholeheartedly to the plan.

You *can* complete these steps—thousands of couples do it every day, just like Tom and Sheila in the Introduction. This book will show you how to get through these steps successfully.

❧ The Benefits of Knowing the Stages and Options

Understanding the stages of relationship development and your action options benefits you in the following ways:

1. It normalizes the stresses, changes, and challenges you face so that you no longer feel like you're different from others or all alone in this.

2. It helps you assess where your marriage currently is so that you know what to expect next and understand the options open to you.

3. It helps you realize that you can make conscious choices about your marital future. You can avoid accepting an unsatisfying but stable marriage when you know you can have much more.

4. It encourages you to make a conscious choice together to do option 3 above rather than option 1 or 2.

Myths About Marriage That Sustain Problems

It's not enough to know that marriage changes over time. Myths about marriage—beliefs we hold as true that have no basis in reality or scientific evidence—also help sustain, and sometimes create, marriage problems. To assess your beliefs in marital myths, rate how much you agree or disagree with each of the statements in Worksheet 1.1.

For each of the myths you agreed with, think of your reasoning in support of the myth. For example, who taught you this myth? What evidence do you have that this myth is true or false? Your belief-in-myths score is high if you agreed or strongly agreed with five or more of the myths. If you agreed or strongly agreed with three or four myths, your score is moderate. Agreeing with two or fewer is a low myth score. The more myths you marked "Undecided" to "Strongly Disagree," the better your understanding of the true nature of marriage and what it takes to be happily married.

Debunking the Myths

Let's go into more detail on these ten myths about marriage. We'll see why each myth is false and provide an alternative, more realistic belief for each myth. I believe that if you can rid yourself of your beliefs in these myths and start thinking more realistically about marriage, you will have taken an important step toward a more satisfying and ultimately easier experience in improving your marriage.

	Strongly Disagree	Disagree	Undecided	Agree	Strongly Agree
Circle Your Responses:					
1. If my spouse loves me, he should *instinctively* know what I want and need to be happy.	1	2	3	4	5
2. No matter how I behave, my spouse should love me simply because she is my spouse.	1	2	3	4	5
3. I can change my spouse by pointing out his inadequacies, errors, and other flaws.	1	2	3	4	5
4. My spouse either loves me or doesn't love me; nothing I do will affect the way she feels about me.	1	2	3	4	5
5. The more my spouse discloses positive and negative information to me, the closer I will feel to her and the greater our marital satisfaction will be.	1	2	3	4	5
6. I must first feel better about my partner before I can change my behavior toward him.	1	2	3	4	5
7. Maintaining romantic love is the key to marital happiness over the life span for most couples.	1	2	3	4	5
8. Marriage should always be a 50–50 partnership.	1	2	3	4	5
9. Marriage can fulfill all of my needs.	1	2	3	4	5
10. Couples should keep their problems to themselves and solve them alone.	1	2	3	4	5

Worksheet 1.1. Beliefs in Marital Myths.[4]

The ESP Myth

The myth: *If my spouse loves me, he should* instinctively *know what I want and need to be happy.*

This is referred to as the ESP or extrasensory perception (mind-reading) myth because it erroneously suggests that spouses can read each other's minds and that only if they do are they really loving people. This is simply not true! Many divorced couples remember saying, "If he had really loved me, he would have *automatically* known what I needed." Research shows that even spouses married for a long time (twenty-five years or more) do not necessarily know or understand each other significantly better than couples married for a shorter period of time. Someone once explained this using a prisoner example: two prisoners may have spent twenty-five years together but still know very little about each other. Might the same not be true of spouses?

The point is, you have to communicate *clearly* about what you want and need from your partner for her to start meeting your needs. And it's not unrealistic to expect to repeat yourself sometimes. This is because all of us have a lot on our minds, along with all those conflicting interests and stresses (kids' needs, boss's needs, and so on).

The reality: *If my spouse really loves me, she will openly and respectfully tell me what she needs and not expect me to read her mind.*

The I'm-Good-Enough-Just-as-I-Am Myth

The myth: *No matter how I behave, my spouse should love me simply because she is my spouse.*

This myth suggests that my own existence regardless of my neglectful, obnoxious, or abusive behavior should make you love me, automatically. I once heard a husband say to his wife in marital therapy, "You should love me for who I am—it's your duty! When you signed that piece of paper [the marriage certificate], you committed to me *regardless* of what I do!" He used this duty statement as a manipulation to keep her in their abusive marriage.

But the fact is, my feelings for you are largely based on how you treat me. If you treat me consistently poorly, don't expect me to love you as a result. I may still be committed to our marriage because I think you can change and become more loving, but don't expect love to come automatically.

The reality: *Your spouse will love you to the extent that you are lovable, and that's based largely on your behavior.*

The Finger-Pointing-Will-Change-Him Myth

The myth: *I can change my spouse by pointing out his inadequacies, errors, and other flaws.*

No one likes to be negatively confronted or blamed. That's human nature. And to be reminded regularly that you're a creep is even worse! The more you remind me of my inadequacies, the less I want to change because after one or two requests, it now becomes a power struggle. This is especially true for husbands. No man likes to think he is controlled by a woman (or anyone else, for that matter!). If you repeatedly hound him (nag), even though he may actually want to change his behavior as you would like him to, he probably will not because then you win and he loses.

Perhaps you have heard the expression "Catch 'em doing something good." Reinforcing positive behavior works better than punishment for negative behavior.

The reality: *I can positively influence my spouse's behavior if I know how, and that can be learned. But nagging does not work.*

The Love-in-a-Vacuum Myth

The myth: *My spouse either loves me or doesn't love me; nothing I do will affect the way she feels about me.*

This myth is similar to "I'm good enough just as I am" in its assumption that feelings and behaviors are separate and unrelated. Spouses who believe this myth are often just using it as an excuse not to change themselves.

The fact is, if I exhibit loving behaviors, her love for me will increase in a reciprocal way. To prove my point, just ask your spouse to complete this sentence: "I feel loved when you (*list ten specific behaviors*)." Then choose one or two of the specific behaviors on the list to start doing sincerely every day for one month. At the end of the month, ask your partner if she feels more love for you. She will. Love does not exist in a vacuum—it is strongly influenced, day to day, by our behavior and our partner's behavior.

The reality: *If I behave more lovingly, she will love me more.*

The Let-It-All-Hang-Out Myth

The myth: *The more my spouse discloses positive and negative information to me, the closer I will feel to her and the greater our marital satisfaction will be.*

So we should tell our partner everything that is on our mind, right? Just let it all hang out. After all, you're soulmates. *Wrong!* Recently, marriage researchers have discovered the "five-to-one rule."[5] This rule holds that for every destructive or hurtful thing I say to my partner, I have to say five positive things to balance the books. That shows that negative comments or disclosures are more emotionally powerful than positive comments or disclosures.

So watch what you disclose to your partner. First, ask yourself, Is telling her this going to seriously hurt her? Is this information that she really doesn't need because it has little influence on our marriage? Here are some examples of things better left undisclosed:

- Something embarrassing from your past that is unrelated to your current relationship—for example, "Last year you really embarrassed me at the company picnic with your silly jokes."

- Negative thoughts or feelings about someone that has no constructive purpose if told to your spouse—for example, "You know, your father is really a slob. I don't know how your mother puts up with him!"

- Unsolicited negative comments about your partner's weight, looks, dress, style, hairdo, and so on. It is better just to pay a compliment when you notice something you like.

The reality: *The expression of positive thoughts and feelings increases marital satisfaction the most. If you have something negative to say, watch how you do it so as not to offend (you'll learn more about this in Chapter Four).*

The My-Feelings-Have-to-Change-First Myth

The myth: *I must first feel better about my partner before I can change my behavior toward him.*

It will be easier to give him more compliments or do him more favors if you first feel more love for him, but how do you change your feelings first? Where is the magic potion? Therapists have little advice on how to feel better first.[6] In comparison, we know a good deal about how to help change your behavior. And it's much more practical to focus on overt behavior first. Besides, the reciprocal relationship between feelings and behavior means that if you change one (behavior), the other (feelings) will change, too. Let me issue this warning: if you wait until you feel better about him first before changing your behavior, you will probably *never* change your behavior!

The reality: *Part of being married is learning that you sometimes have to do things for your partner that you would rather not do, simply to please your partner.[7] As he becomes happier, he will likely reciprocate with pleasing behaviors too, and you, too, will be happier (your feelings change). Plus, you will feel much better about yourself as a result of changing your behavior* first *without hesitating too long.*

The Romantic-Love-Is-the-Key Myth

The myth: *Maintaining romantic love is the key to marital happiness over the life span for most couples.*

Having read my earlier comments about the relative importance of companionate love versus romantic love in preserving long-term marriages, you may not have agreed with this statement. Although maintaining romantic love has some positive effect on long-term marital satisfaction, you need to become friends, preferably before or shortly after marriage. You also need to become more altruistic. These three kinds of love can together preserve your relationship over the life of your marriage.

The reality: *It takes companionate and altruistic love, too, to preserve your marriage.*

The It's-a-50–50-Deal Myth

The myth: *Marriage should always be a 50–50 partnership.*

Unfortunately, circumstances and individuals are too complicated to assume that we can always maintain equal inputs into our marriage. Some days, say, when my wife is sick, I may have to put 90 percent into my marriage while my wife only puts in 10 percent. The next week, that could change to a 10 percent–90 percent ratio due to illnesses, job responsibilities, child-rearing problems, or other circumstances. Over the short term, you cannot have a 50–50 marriage. Over the *long term,* happily married couples report more of a 50–50 contribution to their marriage. In addition, couples who try to split everything equally forget that some things in marriage may be best done by the person who is more competent at it—for example, car repairs may be easy for me but difficult for you. So I'll do all the car repairs. That's fair to both of us but may not reflect a 50–50 marriage as far as car maintenance goes.

The sign of a troubled marriage, incidentally, is when spouses keep tally sheets in their heads, counting everything they do for their partner and resentfully saying, "You owe me!"[8]

The reality: *Your marriage will be stronger if you focus on pleasing your partner and making sure you are doing all you reasonably can to contribute without keeping a tally in your mind.*

The Marriage-Is-the-Ultimate-Answer Myth

The myth: *Marriage can fulfill all of my needs.*

Newly married couples often think this, but after a few months of marriage, they discover the reality that they have many needs and marriage can fulfill only some of them. Each person is responsible for getting those other needs met. For example, a young bride complained that her new husband wouldn't sit and listen to her (endlessly, it seemed to him) at the end of the day and meet her need for meaningful conversation and understanding. He was not used to such long, intimate conversations and quickly tired and eventually got irritated. Luckily, she soon started sharing more of her feelings with close friends, without concluding that her marriage was poor because her husband didn't meet all her needs for conversation.

The fact that you're married does not alter the fact that you should still expect to meet many of your needs outside of marriage, just as before you were married. For example, my need to play golf has never been fulfilled with my wife as my golf partner. She just doesn't like the game. My male buddies do, and so they fill my need for golf course companionship, competition, conversation, and so on.

The reality: *Marriage can fulfill many of my needs, and the others can be fulfilled by other appropriate people.*

The Keep-Quiet-and-Do-It-Alone Myth

The myth: *Couples should keep their problems to themselves and solve them alone.*

This is called the intermarriage taboo.[9] That is, it is taboo to talk to others about your marriage or to seek help outside of marriage. In America we value privacy, but not all cultures do. Too many couples keep their problems to themselves until it is too late—the marriage is so dysfunctional that it's really impossible to repair even by marital therapists. I admire a spirit of independence—we can do it ourselves—but another sign of strength is knowing when to seek outside assistance to improve your marriage. You have shown you already have this strength by reading this book.

There are many loving and professional people ready and willing to help you resolve your marital problems—close family members, friends, clergy, and therapists. Many of our life problems are, after all, solved through others who care. Who cares deeply about you and your marriage who could serve as a sympathetic ear or a source of encouragement or advice? It needs to be a person who can hold confidences like a good friend or a professional. The more objective the person (such as clergy or a marital therapist), the better.

Couples helping couples is an idea developed by Dr. David Mace, the founder of the marriage enrichment movement, and is the philosophy behind his successful marriage enrichment program, called Associated Couples for Marriage Enrichment (ACME).[10] In their couple groups, couples share appropriate problems with one another and get help and support from other couples. These couple groups shatter the myth that you have to keep your problems private and handle them alone. (See their Website, www.bettermarriages.org, for more information on ACME.)

The reality: *Keeping your problems quiet and going it alone often leads to failure. Get trusted others to help you.*

✥ Moving Beyond the Myths: What We Know

Now let's turn to the subject of what we know that predicts marital satisfaction. Chapter Two introduces you to the model I call the *Marriage Triangle*—three key factors that predict your marital satisfaction. The remainder of this book explains the specific subfactors in each of these more general factors that predict marital satisfaction. It also gives you the opportunity to assess yourself and your relationship on each of these important points and to set goals for improvement in yourself and your relationship. At the end of the book, in Chapters Six and Seven, I'll show you how to bring all these factors and your assessments together to improve your marriage.

The Marriage Triangle

Three Factors That Predict Your Marital Satisfaction

You're unsatisfied with your marriage: it's not living up to its potential, and you're not going to just stand by and let things worsen. So you talk to trusted people and other resources in your life, seeking advice on what to do:

- The article in your favorite relationships magazine says good communication is "the key."
- Your mother tells you that your psychological health is most significant.
- Your clergyperson reminds you it's commitment that makes the biggest difference.
- The Beatles assure you, "All you need is love."

Everyone has advice for married couples these days. The problem is that none of this advice is totally correct—nor is it totally incorrect.

So what factors best predict or explain your level of marital satisfaction? What factors are easier or more difficult to work on? How does your marriage compare to others' in terms of overall satisfaction? Where do you start in assessing the condition of your marriage?

In writing this book, I wanted to share with you the predictors of marital satisfaction that social science researchers have found to be reliable over the past fifty years. I am not a pop psychologist with my own biased set of ideas on what predicts marital satisfaction but in fact a researcher and therapist at a major university with twenty-two years of experience in doing marital therapy, researching the scientific literature, and conducting my own research on predictors of marital satisfaction.

Based on a comprehensive review of the literature and my own most recent original research using a new scientific questionnaire called the RELATionship Evaluation, or RELATE,[1] I will provide you with the latest information on the factors and issues that will help you determine the condition of your marriage and how to improve it. As you read this book, you, too, will have the opportunity to take the most important parts of the RELATE test and other scientifically validated questions to obtain expert guidance for your own situation.

𝔤 Where the Research Came From

Over the past eight years, family scientist Dr. Tom Holman and I have conducted an exhaustive review of the social science research literature on characteristics that predict marital satisfaction. In reviewing clinical and research literature from about 1950 to the present, we found over two dozen specific factors that contribute to marital satisfaction. We grouped these characteristics (for example, individual psychological health and communication skills) into three general, major factors: context, individual traits, and couple traits. These three major factors make up the Marriage Triangle.

We also have conducted new longitudinal research on the predictors of marital satisfaction using the Marriage Triangle and RELATE. This recent research has verified and clarified the importance of each of the three major factors in the triangle and the multiple subfactors in each dimension in the prediction of marital satisfaction.[2] The validity and reliability of the RELATE questionnaire items have also been verified.[3]

The Three Factors

After reviewing the literature and conducting our research, we found that the two dozen or so specific predictors could be logically categorized into a triangular model of three major factors.[4]

- Your individual and relationship *contexts* including family-of-origin experiences and current stress levels.

- Your *individual traits* including your personality, attitudes, and skills.

- Your *couple traits*—couple communication, sexual adjustment, conflict resolution skills, and so on.

Figure 2.1 presents these factors in graphic form.

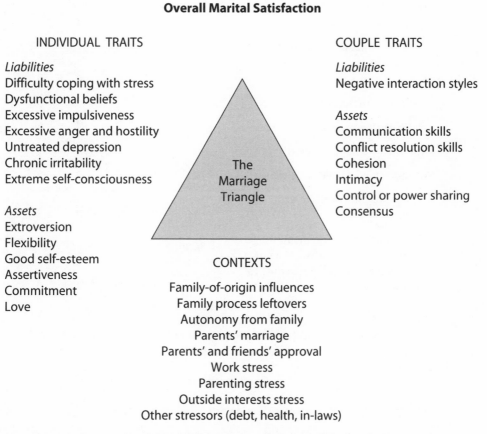

Overall Marital Satisfaction

INDIVIDUAL TRAITS

Liabilities
Difficulty coping with stress
Dysfunctional beliefs
Excessive impulsiveness
Excessive anger and hostility
Untreated depression
Chronic irritability
Extreme self-consciousness

Assets
Extroversion
Flexibility
Good self-esteem
Assertiveness
Commitment
Love

The Marriage Triangle

COUPLE TRAITS

Liabilities
Negative interaction styles

Assets
Communication skills
Conflict resolution skills
Cohesion
Intimacy
Control or power sharing
Consensus

CONTEXTS
Family-of-origin influences
Family process leftovers
Autonomy from family
Parents' marriage
Parents' and friends' approval
Work stress
Parenting stress
Outside interests stress
Other stressors (debt, health, in-laws)

Figure 2.1. The Marriage Triangle: Major Factors and Subfactors.

For an introduction to these three factors, first answer the questions on Worksheet 2.1. These are examples of questions from the RELATE instrument that you will also respond to later in Chapters Three through Five.

	Circle Your Responses:				
	Strongly Disagree	Disagree	Undecided	Agree	Strongly Agree
1. There are matters from my family of origin that I'm still having trouble dealing with and am coming to terms with.	1	2	3	4	5
2. I would like my marriage to be like my parents' marriage.	1	2	3	4	5
3. My parents encourage me to be independent and make my own decisions.	1	2	3	4	5
4. I feel I am a person of worth.	1	2	3	4	5
5. I avoid getting mad or irritated.	1	2	3	4	5
6. I am usually a happy person.	1	2	3	4	5
7. We understand each other's feelings.	1	2	3	4	5
8. I struggle to find words to express myself to my spouse.	1	2	3	4	5
9. When we are in an argument, we recognize when we are overwhelmed and then make a deliberate effort to calm ourselves down.	1	2	3	4	5

Scoring: To score this worksheet, first, reverse the score for items 1 and 8. For example, if you circled 1, score it as 5; if you circled 2, score it as 4; 3 remains the same. Then sum your responses as follows:

1. Sum your responses to items 1–3, and write your answer here: _____

2. Sum your responses to items 4–6, and write your answer here: _____

3. Sum your responses to items 7–9, and write your answer here: _____

Worksheet 2.1. Examples of RELATE Questions.[5]

Items 1–3 measure your perceptions of some of the characteristics in your individual context—family-of-origin experiences that still trouble you, your parents' marital satisfaction, and your autonomy in your family. Your score may range from 3 (lowest) to 15 (highest). This score is a rough indicator of your overall satisfaction with your family-of-origin experiences.

Items 4–6 are measures of your individual traits, including self-esteem, anger management, and happiness. Again, scores may range from 3 to 15 and reflect your perception of your overall mental health.

Items 7–9 are measures of your perceived couple traits, more specifically, communication and conflict resolution skills. Scores range from 3 to 15 and reflect the overall quality of your couple communication skills.

A total score below 9 on one of these short three-item tests suggests a potential problem in that area of the Marriage Triangle. For example, a total score of 7 on items 7–9 indicates poor couple communication or conflict resolution skills. In which area—contexts, individual traits, or couple traits—did you score the highest? The lowest? Why? These questions and scoring guidelines are generalizations because to assess each factor in the triangle comprehensively requires answering more questions from each area in the triangle. You will do that in Chapters Three, Four, and Five. These short tests are presented now simply as an introduction to the three factors in the triangle. Now let's look more closely at each factor.

Personal and Relationship Contexts

Personal context characteristics include family-of-origin influences, such as the degree of love and unity in the family in which you grew up, the quality of your parents' marriage, and your degree of autonomy in your family of origin.

Relationship context refers to the situation or environment in which your relationship currently exists. Examples of relationship context factors include support from in-laws, chronically unresolved marital problems, and stress caused by spending too much time or energy in raising children, dealing with financial problems, and so on.

Personal and relationship contexts are purposely placed at the base or foundation of the Marriage Triangle. This is because your experiences in your family of origin and your continuing relationship with your parents form the basis or foundation of your personality (individual traits) and couple interaction skills (couple traits), which are assets or liabilities in your marriage.

Stresses in your relationship context may be piling up and negatively affecting your marriage, too. Unresolved, chronic financial problems make you anxious and depressed and strain your ability to communicate. Lack of support from in-laws hurts your marriage by demoralizing you. The stronger the base of your Marriage Triangle, the better your marriage will be. Fortunately, weaknesses resulting from problems in this base can be overcome. In this book you will assess the factors in your own base and learn ways to overcome weaknesses traced back to this base.

Individual Traits

The second major factor in predicting success in marriage is your *individual traits,* including your personality, attitudes, and skills. The specific subfactors that make up this factor are as follows:

Traits That Predict Marital Dissatisfaction	Traits That Predict Marital Satisfaction
Difficulty coping with stress	Extroversion
Dysfunctional beliefs	Flexibility
Excessive impulsiveness	Good self-esteem
Excessive anger and hostility	Good interpersonal skills (such as assertiveness)
Untreated depression	Commitment
Chronic irritability	Love
Extreme self-consciousness	

These personality characteristics are related to marital dysfunction (for example, impulsivity) as well as to marital satisfaction (for example, flexibility). For an example of how a personality trait can harm marital satisfaction, consider the characteristic of impulsiveness. Impulsive people often act before thinking. They fail to first consider the consequences of their actions on themselves or others. This may cause marital problems if, for example, the impulsive partner goes out and overspends on a credit card without first considering if the couple can afford the purchases.

In a recent marital therapy session, a wife complained to me that her husband had gone out and charged his VISA card to its maximum level by purchasing appliances and furniture for their new apartment. He reported, "All the stuff was on sale, honey! I just couldn't pass it up!" He hadn't discussed the purchases with her before buying these items, nor had he first thought about their budget, which was tight. She was rightfully resentful. His impulsivity got both of them into financial trouble.

The role of each personality trait in harming or enhancing your marriage will be described more thoroughly in Chapter Four. A relevant term in connection with this is *emotional health.* Emotional health is measured mainly by the presence or absence of abnormally high anxiety, depression, and anger. It should be easy to see why having a spouse who is significantly depressed (that is, struggling with more than the normal blues we all experience now and then) leads to problems in marriage—problems that include reduced communication, a poor sex life, and a lack of positive shared experiences. You will learn more about these personality traits and their role in marital satisfaction in Chapter Four.

Self-esteem and self-confidence also play a major role in marital satisfaction. People with high self-esteem and self-confidence are more likely to be unselfish, considerate of others, and supportive of others. Low self-esteem leads to the opposite conditions: selfishness, inconsiderateness, and an inability to provide emotional support to others. You will have the opportunity to evaluate your self-esteem as part of your self-assessment in Chapter Four.

Everyone agrees that marriage is a stressful relationship. No wonder individuals who have difficulty coping with stress report more marital dissatisfaction. The additional stress of making a living, paying bills, and maintaining a household require you to learn good stress management skills. You can take positive steps to keep stress from taking over your life—like Joan, who told me, "Before I see Steve after work, I first get relaxed. I learned that listening to classical music on the way home from work and then drinking a soda and reading the paper before he got home really mellows me. Then I can handle the rest of the evening with Steve."

Dysfunctional beliefs are another component of the individual traits factor. Dysfunctional beliefs we have identified that have a strong negative effect on marital satisfaction include "People cannot change" and "Disagreement in a relationship is bad." Chapter Four discusses in more detail these and other dysfunctional beliefs that can damage your marriage.

Two personality traits that are resources in marriage are extroversion (sometimes referred to as *sociability*) and assertiveness. People who are extroverted and assertive are more likely to have the communication and conflict management skills necessary to maintain long-term, close personal relationships with others. They are more likely than introverted or nonassertive individuals to be open in their communication with others and understand others' thoughts and feelings. Such relationship maintenance skills are valuable resources in marriage. As Claudia (twenty-five) said of her husband, David (twenty-six): "I'm so glad David is outgoing and open with his feelings. It keeps us from misunderstanding each other. Instead, we can solve the problems as they come up. I never wonder what he's thinking or feeling. He tells me!"

Finally, your feelings of love and commitment for your partner are major predictors of your marital satisfaction. However, love and commitment are separate phenomena. *Love* as defined here has three components: (1) a sense of emotional attachment to your partner ("I miss her when she's not here"), (2) the experience of intimacy with her ("I can tell her important things about me"), and (3) caring ("I want to do things for her"). Later you will assess these three components of love currently in your marriage.

Commitment refers to your perception of the permanence of your relationship, your avoidance of involvement in other romantic relationships, and the anticipation of loss if the marriage were to end. Although love and commitment usually go hand in hand, they may not. For example, you may not love your partner very much but still feel committed to staying with him due to strong religious beliefs about the permanence of marriage, the lack of good alternative relationships, or the threat of loss of financial security or emotional support if a divorce occurred. You will also rate your current level of commitment to your marriage.

Couple Traits

The third major predictive factor is your *couple traits.* These consist of your couple communication and conflict resolution skills, cohesion, intimacy, control or power, and consensus. The better your communication and conflict resolution skills, the better you resolve differences and manage your life together. Of all the factors discussed in this book, communication and conflict resolution skills are two of the most important predictors of marital satisfaction. With good communication skills, love, and a kind attitude, many marital conflicts, values differences, and dissimilarities can be resolved successfully.

Communication skills, therefore, are the oil in the marriage engine. Without them, the engine runs poorly or not at all. Students in my marriage enrichment course have made comments like these about communication in their marriages:

"My husband is a great listener. I know after a difficult conversation that he has understood how I feel. That's how we solve all our conflicts."

"The speaking skills I have learned in this course are especially helpful to my husband and me. Before learning them, I had no idea why he was so frustrated with me when I would go off on him. Now I can more calmly state my feelings, thoughts, and needs, so he is less confused and overwhelmed."

More details on assessing communication and conflict resolution skills in your relationship are presented in Chapter Five.

There are four additional important relationship dimensions: cohesion, intimacy, control or power, and consensus. Let us examine them one by one.

Cohesion

A major hurdle for all couples early in marriage is to figure out how much time to spend together and how much time to spend apart. The more time enjoyably spent together, the greater the cohesion. But being married does not mean you have to give up all the individual interests, hobbies, and activities you enjoyed when you were single. You many have to cut back some, but don't give them up entirely. In fact, a warning light should go off when your partner in a relationship demands that you give up all your hobbies and activities just to be with her. That's called possessiveness, and it only leads to trouble.

At the same time, as a wife said in a therapy session, "I didn't marry him to stay home alone!" Efforts at balancing aloneness and togetherness should be expected, especially early in marriage. My wife and I find it comfortable to have a lady's night out and a gentleman's night out each week—one night a week alone while the other cares for the kids. I go to the movies she doesn't like (usually testosterone-laden action films) or eat at my favorite spot without worrying about compromising with her, or I just listen to my kind of music, most of which she doesn't like (1960's rock-and-roll). On her night alone, she runs errands I'd rather not be on with her (to fabric shops, for example), goes to her choice of a movie, visits the library, or whatever else she wants to do. We also share many experiences and activities together—we go to some movies together, go out for dinner together, and attend concerts and other events. It took us several years to finally work out a balance between aloneness and togetherness that is custom-fit for us.

Intimacy

People marry to be intimate. But what does intimacy mean? Intimacy in marriage encompasses several things:

- Self-disclosure—closeness resulting from sharing feelings, thoughts, needs, fears, plans, and so on

- Affection—nonsexual hugs, holding hands, expressions of love, cards, flowers, and the like

- Sexual intercourse—enough said!

- Cohesion or unity—a source of "we-ness" and emotional closeness resulting from common values, similar goals, togetherness, and enjoying each other's company

Using the assessments in this book, you will find out whether your marriage is high, medium, or low on each of these dimensions of intimacy. When you break down intimacy into these more simple concepts, it's easier to assess yourselves and set goals for improvement. Adding your scores on all these dimensions will provide an overall sense of the depth of intimacy in your marriage.

Control or Power Sharing

A major important dimension in all human relationships is control or power. *Power* is defined here as the ability to influence another person to go in the direction *you* want. You have heard of power struggles in marriage. Power struggles in marriage usually focus on how money is spent, conflict resolution, and how important decisions are made ("who's wearing the pants" in the marriage). It's not the topic of debate that is important, it's *how it is discussed* (conflict resolution skills) and *how power is shared.* An imbalance of power—the tendency of one spouse to exercise too much power or control in decision making—has been dubbed the "tyranny trap" by Dr. Brent Barlow.[6]

"The question of who has the right to do what to whom and when is the pervasive, nagging issue which must be worked out by every couple, for it arises daily. A set of relationship rules must be agreed upon. In the formulation of these rules, each individual must feel that he has a right, equal to the other's right to determine what goes on."[7]

Power problems affect other areas in your marriage, too. They show up most clearly in your sexual relationship—that is, power issues end up in bed. For example, rare is the wife who would feel attracted to or seek sexual relations with a husband who earlier in the evening made an important decision without consulting her, claiming that he has the right to make final decisions on his own. In such a circumstance, I'd feel angry and resentful; I'd feel that I'd been taken advantage of; I'd feel that I had not been treated fairly. Those feelings are not great aphrodisiacs! Unfortunately, sometimes withholding sex is used as a weapon against a spouse who is perceived to be exercising too much power. That tactic should be recognized as a reflection that the withholder is feeling put upon or put down.

Consensus

Consensus refers to the degree of agreement you and your partner experience on a variety of marital issues such as proper behavior in public, religious matters, decision making, and displays of affection. The more you agree on these issues, the higher your consensus. The more consensus, the easier it is to get along, and the smoother the marriage functions.

However, it is not uncommon for couples to lack consensus on some marital issues. If you have good communication skills, a loving attitude, and a certain level of tolerance, you can learn to adjust to most differences. For example, successful interfaith couples learn how to agree to disagree. As a result, partners may each attend their own church services. However, when children are born, a loving attitude and good conflict resolution skills are required to reach a mutually agreed decision or consensus about the children's religious training.

Consensus can be realized in one of three ways in marriage: (1) you accept and appreciate that you are already similar, (2) you accept your differences without resentment or despair, or (3) you reach consensus through healthy conflict resolution. In your marriage you may expect to use all three of these consensus-building strategies, although you will find that you use one more than the others. The more differences between you when you marry, the more likely you will need to use strategies 2 and 3.

How the Factors Work Together

An example of how these three general factors work together to affect marital satisfaction or dissatisfaction will be helpful. Ann grew up in a dysfunctional family in which there was high conflict and low cohesion or unity. She seldom felt loved or accepted by her parents (a context factor at the base of the Marriage Triangle). Thus her self-esteem suffered throughout her life, and she was often depressed (individual traits). These problems then negatively influenced her decision of both whom to marry—she married a man who had very different values but gave her the attention she had always craved—and *when* to marry—she married hurriedly after knowing him only two months. Her depression hampered her in the marriage by negatively affecting communication and conflict resolution skills (couple traits). It also caused her to seldom want to be together with her husband (couple trait). She never sought education or treatment for her problems. Ann and her husband divorced after three years.

Each of the subfactors listed in Figure 2.1 and its potential influence on your marital satisfaction will be described in the remainder of this book, and you will have the opportunity to assess yourself, your relationship, and your contexts to determine how each one is influencing your marital satisfaction.

The first impression you may have after reviewing this list is that predicting marital satisfaction is more complicated than you originally thought! The purpose of this book is to uncomplicate prediction and help you conduct a comprehensive marital checkup and then decide how to perform a marital tune-up.

Be assured that you and your partner do *not* have to be perfect in order to have a successful marriage! Marriage is a risk—and a formula for success—for all couples, of any sort. This book will help you lower your risk of dissatisfaction and divorce and increase your chances of satisfaction and stability. You will do this, first, by learning about the factors that predict a successful marriage; second, by assessing the strengths and weaknesses of yourself, your relationship, and the contexts in which you live; and third, by setting goals and engaging in self- and couple-oriented activities to tune up your marriage.

Assessment and the Marriage Triangle

The assessments in this book are basically short tests or measures (usually consisting of three or four questions) of important factors in the Marriage Triangle. For example, the assessment of your self-esteem consists of three items that can be answered in about ten seconds. Directions for scoring each short test are included at the end of each chapter. Norm scores (national averages) are provided so that you can compare your scores to those of other married adults (aged eighteen to sixty-five) who have completed the short tests. These comparisons will give you an idea of your relative strengths and weaknesses. Most norm scores come from a data bank consisting of over two thousand married couples who have taken the RELATE test since 1997. Finally, discussion questions based on your results are included at the end of each chapter to help you better understand your strengths and weaknesses and to help you set goals on how to improve yourself and your relationship.

Note that the assessments are only as valid as you are honest in completing them. Try to be as objective as you can in answering each item. The most important part of the assessment process is discussing what the results mean to you and your partner. Take time to enjoy and take pleasure in your high scores—these scores identify some of the strengths in yourself or your relationship. Look at the areas where you have low scores and discuss their implications.

On these short tests you may find that some of your scores are rather low. Your first reaction may be to ignore or deny the differences. Instead, you should meet this challenge head-on. To help you do this, here are some suggestions about how to discuss these issues.[8]

First, look at your differences and weaknesses honestly and openly. It is usually better to face your differences and weaknesses than to deny them or try to avoid them. Find some time when you can discuss these things in one or more long, uninterrupted sessions. Try to determine what is really going on in that aspect of yourself or your relationship. This process requires the application of communication and problem-solving skills in a loving environment to iron out the differences and set goals for turning weaknesses into strengths in an appropriate manner. Therefore, allow some time to do it; be patient and be a good listener, and try to empathize with your partner's perceptions too.

Second, remember that some of the short-test results you may need to discuss with your partner are sensitive (for example, family background) and may affect your own feelings of self-worth. Ask your partner to be supportive and considerate as you discuss these results. If you become threatened, slow down or even stop and deal with the feelings that are occurring.

Third, if some problematic test results cause you great concern, consider seeking assistance in dealing with those problems by sharing your results with a licensed marital therapist and getting help in interpreting your test results and deciding the best course of action.

In summary, you will evaluate your own Marriage Triangle as you read this book. The triangle corresponds to three levels of a relationship (see Figure 2.2). As described earlier, each level has its own set of influences. Unfortunately, social scientists do not yet agree on which level of the relationship or which factor in the triangle best explains why some couples remain happily married while others do not. The most important thing is to be complete in your assessment of these three levels and then decide where your marriage needs to be tuned up.

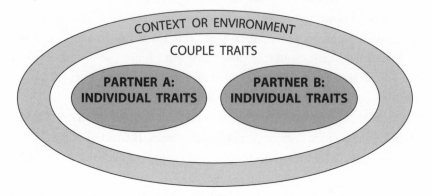

Figure 2.2. Three Levels of a Relationship.[9]

Using the Rest of This Book

The next three chapters give more detailed descriptions of the three factors in the Marriage Triangle and self-assessments on each set of factors. For example, after reading about how self-esteem and personality affect marriage, you will assess your level of self-esteem and several personality characteristics. You will then answer a series of questions about your results and be asked to discuss some of them with your partner.

By the end of these assessments and discussions, you will have completed a thorough and meaningful set of assessment exercises that will serve to answer such questions as these:

- How satisfied are we with our marriage?
- What individual and couple strengths serve to enhance our marriage?
- What individual and couple weaknesses limit our chances of a successful marriage?

- What contexts are assets or liabilities for our marriage? How can we deal with them more effectively?

- What are our individual and couple goals for improving our marriage?

- Where can we get more assistance for improving our marriage? For overcoming personal problems? Couple problems? Context problems?

In Chapter Three you begin the assessment process by assessing your personal strengths and liabilities. This assessment is done first to emphasize that it takes two healthy individuals to make a healthy partnership. Remember to be open and honest in assessing yourself, for only then can you benefit from this process.

THREE

Factor 1

Your Individual Traits

John tries to keep the peace at all costs! He seems to think that any disagreement we have means we have a bad marriage. It's like he's conflict-phobic.

—Mary, fifty-two-year-old professor

Tom is such a steady, easygoing husband. He seldom gets all wound up. That helps us maintain balance in our marriage and deal with stress.

—Margaret, thirty-two-year-old homemaker

Jaimee has poor self-esteem—always has. I easily offend her as a result, and she can hold a grudge for days.

—Don, twenty-nine-year-old salesman

If Tim weren't so flexible in his attitude about things, we could never compromise. And compromising is the heart of marriage.

—Emily, forty-year-old nurse

These statements by married individuals demonstrate the importance to a marriage of good emotional health and functional beliefs. Marriage experts say, "A good marriage begins with the individual." The purpose of this chapter is to show you how certain personality traits in you and your partner and certain beliefs about relationships affect the way you relate to each other, handle stress, become intimate, resolve problems, and experience marital satisfaction or dissatisfaction. In this chapter I use research findings to answer two important questions:

1. What personality traits and attitudes are related to marital dissatisfaction and satisfaction?

2. What types of functional and dysfunctional beliefs about your relationship are related to dissatisfaction and satisfaction?

These individual traits directly affect the other two legs of the Marriage Triangle. For example, if I'm depressed and anxious, I will not resolve problems well with my wife (couple trait). If I am vulnerable to stress, I won't deal well with stress that affects marriage (context trait). Alternatively, if I have good self-esteem and I am assertive, I will communicate with my partner more clearly and deal appropriately with in-law issues (context trait).

Simply stated, without healthy personality traits, attitudes, and beliefs, you may be a person who is difficult to live with. As marital researcher Laurence Kurdek said so well, personality traits may predispose a partner to distort relationship events or to overreact to negative relationship events. Certain traits may thus contribute to one's being very difficult to live with.[1]

Let's see an example of this. Tina (thirty-five) had low self-esteem and chronic depression from growing up in an abusive family. She had many self-doubts—she doubted that her husband really loved her. She often wondered if he was more attracted to other women. She was often jealous and almost paranoid about it. Reassurances from him did not seem to help. Her basic lack of self-worth and her depressed state caused her to blow up at him anytime she felt threatened by another woman, which turned out to be practically every time he had dealings with other women, including his fellow workers and his clients. As a result, he became very frustrated with her and started developing some symptoms of depression, too. This is common in marriages where one person is clinically depressed. It's called depression contagion. Her depression was contagious, and he was catching it! No wonder marital therapy is helpful when one's spouse suffers from depression. By the way, depression is the common cold of all emotional problems—over twenty million Americans have it at any given time, and few get treatment for it. Individual traits are like the nucleus of a cell, as shown in Figure 2.2. Each partner's individual traits interact with the other's in a systemic manner. So for your marriage to thrive, it is vital that you and your partner be emotionally healthy.

Before going any further, let's do an assessment of some of your key individual traits. Please complete and score the short tests in Worksheet 3.1. At the end of the chapter I'll interpret the meanings of these scores.

	Never	Rarely	Sometimes	Often	Very Often
					Circle Your Responses:

Personality Traits

In items 1–32, answer how well these words describe you now:

	Never	Rarely	Sometimes	Often	Very Often
1. Talkative	1	2	3	4	5
2. Quiet	1	2	3	4	5
3. Shy	1	2	3	4	5
4. Outgoing	1	2	3	4	5

Reverse-score items 2 and 3. For example, if you circled 1, score it as 5; if you circled 2, score it as 4; 3 remains the same. Then sum your responses to items 1–4, and write your score here: _____

	Never	Rarely	Sometimes	Often	Very Often
5. Worried	1	2	3	4	5
6. Fearful	1	2	3	4	5
7. Tense	1	2	3	4	5
8. Nervous	1	2	3	4	5

Sum your responses to items 5–8, and write your score here: _____

	Never	Rarely	Sometimes	Often	Very Often
9. Open-minded	1	2	3	4	5
10. Flexible	1	2	3	4	5
11. Easygoing	1	2	3	4	5
12. Adaptable	1	2	3	4	5

Sum your responses to items 9–12, and write your score here: _____

	Never	Rarely	Sometimes	Often	Very Often
13. Fight with others, lose temper	1	2	3	4	5
14. Act immature under pressure	1	2	3	4	5
15. Easily irritated or mad	1	2	3	4	5

Sum your responses to items 13–15, and write your score here: _____

Worksheet 3.1. Assessing Personality Traits.

	Never	Rarely	Sometimes	Often	Very Often
					Circle Your Responses:
16. Sad and blue	1	2	3	4	5
17. Hopeless	1	2	3	4	5
18. Depressed	1	2	3	4	5

Sum your responses to items 16–18, and write your score here: _____

	Never	Rarely	Sometimes	Often	Very Often
19. Impulsive	1	2	3	4	5
20. Act before thinking first	1	2	3	4	5
21. Easily tempted	1	2	3	4	5

Sum your responses to items 19–21, and write your score here: _____

	Never	Rarely	Sometimes	Often	Very Often
22. Deal well with stress	1	2	3	4	5
23. Fall apart in a crisis	1	2	3	4	5
24. Helpless under pressure	1	2	3	4	5

Reverse-score item 22. Then sum your responses to items 22–24, and write your score here: _____

	Never	Rarely	Sometimes	Often	Very Often
25. Speak up in a crowd	1	2	3	4	5
26. Tell it like it is	1	2	3	4	5
27. Say what I really think	1	2	3	4	5
28. Assertive	1	2	3	4	5

Sum your responses to items 25–28, and write your score here: _____

	Never	Rarely	Sometimes	Often	Very Often
29. Take a positive attitude toward myself	1	2	3	4	5
30. Think I am not good at all	1	2	3	4	5
31. Feel I am a person of worth	1	2	3	4	5
32. Think I am a failure	1	2	3	4	5

Reverse-score items 30 and 32. Then sum your responses to items 29–32, and write your score here: _____

Worksheet 3.1. Assessing Personality Traits, *Continued*

	Circle Your Responses:				
	Never	*Rarely*	*Sometimes*	*Often*	*Very Often*

Love[2]

33. I show a lot of love toward my partner. — 1 2 3 4 5

34. One of my primary concerns is my partner's welfare. — 1 2 3 4 5

35. It would be hard for me to get along without my partner. — 1 2 3 4 5

Sum your responses to items 33–35, and write your score here: _____

	Circle Your Responses:				
	Strongly Disagree	*Disagree*	*Undecided*	*Agree*	*Strongly Agree*

Commitment

36. My relationship with my partner is clearly part of my future plans. — 1 2 3 4 5

37. I want this relationship to stay strong no matter what rough times we may encounter. — 1 2 3 4 5

38. I may not want to be with my partner a few years from now. — 1 2 3 4 5

Reverse-score item 38. Then sum your responses to items 36–38, and write your score here: _____

39. My partner or I have an emotional or personal problem that should be treated by a professional (for example, depression, phobia, anxiety, eating disorder, alcoholism). — Yes No Unsure

40. My partner or I have a serious, chronic physical health problem that should be treated by a professional (for example, ulcer, diabetes, handicap, chronic fatigue). — Yes No Unsure

Worksheet 3.1. Assessing Personality Traits, *Continued*

	Strongly Disagree	Disagree	Undecided	Agree	Strongly Agree

Circle Your Responses:

Beliefs About Individuals or Relationships

Rate the extent to which you agree with the following statements.

41. If your partner disagrees with your ideas, he or she probably does not think highly of you.	1	2	3	4	5
42. I cannot accept it when my partner disagrees with me.	1	2	3	4	5
43. I take it as a personal insult when my partner disagrees with an important idea of mine.	1	2	3	4	5

Sum your responses to items 41–43, and write your score here: _____

44. I get very upset if my partner does not recognize how I am feeling and I have to tell him or her.	1	2	3	4	5
45. People who have a close relationship can sense each other's needs as if they could read each other's minds.	1	2	3	4	5
46. It is important to me for my partner to anticipate my needs by sensing changes in my moods.	1	2	3	4	5

Sum your responses to items 44–46, and write your score here: _____

47. My partner does not seem capable of behaving other than he or she does now.	1	2	3	4	5
48. A partner who hurts you badly once will probably hurt you again.	1	2	3	4	5
49. I do not expect my partner to be able to change.	1	2	3	4	5

Sum your responses to items 46–49, and write your score here: _____

Worksheet 3.1. Assessing Personality Traits, *Continued*

	Strongly Disagree	Disagree	Undecided	Agree	Strongly Agree
50. A good sexual partner can get himself or herself aroused for sex whenever necessary.	1	2	3	4	5
51. If I cannot perform well sexually whenever my partner is in the mood, I would consider that I have a problem.	1	2	3	4	5
52. Some difficulties in my sexual performance mean personal failure to me.	1	2	3	4	5

Sum your responses to items 50–52, and write your score here: _____

	Strongly Disagree	Disagree	Undecided	Agree	Strongly Agree
53. Misunderstandings between partners are generally due to inborn differences in the psychological makeup of men and women.	1	2	3	4	5
54. You can't really understand someone of the opposite sex.	1	2	3	4	5
55. One of the major causes of marital problems is that men and women have different emotional needs.	1	2	3	4	5

Sum your responses to items 53–55, and write your score here: _____

Worksheet 3.1. Assessing Personality Traits, *Continued*

✌ Traits That Cause Marriage Problems

The following six personality traits are related to marital dissatisfaction:

- Vulnerability to stress
- Impulsiveness
- Anger and hostility
- Depression
- Anxiety
- Self-consciousness

These six personality traits are referred to as neurotic traits.[3] All of us have a certain measure of these traits naturally; they are part of being human. For example, "rainy days and Mondays always get me down." And sometimes I am impulsive and buy something I shouldn't; later I feel guilty (especially if my wife comments on it!). But excessive amounts of these traits are unhealthy and cause marriage problems. Let's look at some examples.

Vulnerability to Stress

Excessive vulnerability to stress can cause special problems. Marriage is a stressful relationship involving the juggling of schedules, unexpected crises, sacrifices that have to be made that inconvenience us, conflicts that must be resolved, and so on. Marriage is not for the faint of heart! The less vulnerable you are to everyday stress, the less negatively your marriage is affected. Fortunately, vulnerability to stress can be overcome through stress management techniques.

Impulsiveness

Excessive impulsiveness negatively affects the family budget or other plans. Going to play golf on the spur of the moment is great fun and should occasionally be done, but if it becomes a habit, my boss is upset, my wife's plans are interrupted, work doesn't get done, and so forth. Impulsive spending especially causes problems and is the most dangerous kind of impulsive behavior in marriage. It can lead to resentment in your spouse, marital conflict, guilt for you, and financial stress.

Anger and Hostility

Excessively angry and hostile people are difficult to cope with. Such spouses regularly hurt their partner's feelings, create an atmosphere of negativity and fear in the home, cause resentment in family members, and cause people to disconnect emotionally. Anger inhibits productive conflict resolution. It ruins your sex life. Most dangerous of all, it may lead to verbal or physical abuse. Simply put, excessive anger poisons a marriage. Fortunately, we can all learn to control and manage our anger in ways that prevent damage to our marriage.

Depression

Untreated depression brings the whole marriage down. I'm convinced that it works both ways. First, when you're clinically depressed, you are handicapped in performing your marital role. It's like playing football with one good leg: you don't get very far. Second, marriage problems cause depression, sometimes to the point of clinical depression, which should be treated directly with antidepressants, individual psychotherapy, and marital therapy. There is much your spouse can do to help alleviate your symptoms—including offering sincere compliments, assisting with housework, encouragement, patience, adjusting her expectations to a more reasonable level.

Anxiety

Excessive and chronic anxiety takes a toll on marriage. It usually takes the forms of excessive worry, uneasiness without knowing why, irritability, nervousness, shakiness, and an inability to relax. It negatively affects your ability to communicate and resolve conflict with your spouse, make decisions, and have fun together. It is an enemy to your sex life—reducing your libido and decreasing your pleasure. Depression, by the way, does the same things to your sex life as anxiety. Often anxiety and depression occur together. Again, medications and therapy are usually the best solution, barring physical causes of these emotional problems.

Self-Consciousness

A self-conscious spouse will drive you crazy. She will relentlessly ask for your opinion on her weight, her looks, her dress, her style, and everything else. Your reassurances will not be accepted because she does not believe you or anyone else. This happens because the source of self-consciousness is much deeper. Excessively self-conscience people have poor self-esteem in the first place. They think others are looking at them critically. For example, have you ever walked by a group of individuals when just as you do they begin to laugh? The self-conscience person swears they are laughing at him. He thinks, "I probably have my zipper down" or "They think I'm a geek." Little does he realize that a joke was just being told as he walked by and two of the women actually thought he was handsome as they noticed him walking by. For the self-conscious person, the glass is always half-empty. Self-consciousness can also be overcome with psychotherapy.

Notice that many of these six traits occur together in the same individual. For example, depressed people usually have low self-esteem and are anxious. They are often vulnerable to stress. And someone who doesn't handle stress well may become irritable, angry, and hostile. These emotions are understandably linked.

Let me reiterate that low or occasionally moderate levels of these neurotic traits are part of being a human being. To some degree, neurotic is normal! It's when these traits are exaggerated for long periods of time or when they significantly affect our functioning as a spouse, employee, or student that we need to be concerned. At the end of this chapter I will explain how to determine if your scores on these traits are abnormally high and what to do next if they are.

The Role of Dysfunctional Beliefs

Certain types of dysfunctional beliefs also add to marital dissatisfaction. Beliefs about marriage and my partner are very influential in determining how I act toward and feel about my partner. Beliefs or expectations are the standards I use to evaluate my marriage, myself, and my partner. Dysfunctional beliefs are those that are constraining. "Constraining beliefs perpetuate problems and restrict options for alternative solutions to problems. Facilitative (or functional) beliefs increase options for solutions to problems."[4]

Researchers have identified five beliefs that are dysfunctional or constraining:[5]

1. *Disagreement is destructive.* Believing that "disagreement means you have a bad marriage" or that "disagreements will destroy your marriage" are unrealistic and constraining. They will keep you from directly and honestly facing areas of disagreement in marriage and resolving them.

2. *Partners are mind readers.* Beliefs such as "If you really loved me, you would automatically know what I need to be happy" or "You should know what I want without my saying it" reflect the ESP myth. The truth is, most of us cannot read our partner's mind. Instead, we must rely on our partner's telling us what he or she needs or wants.

3. *A partner cannot change.* Examples of this belief are reflected in statements like "People don't really change all that much over time" or "My partner is incapable of changing." Such beliefs inhibit us from asking our partner for change and lead to discouragement, frustration, and resentment. Fortunately, people *can* and *do* change.

4. *Sexual perfection is possible.* Believing that "there is only one right way to have sex" or that "only if we achieve orgasm at the same time can we be satisfied" exemplify this type of perfectionism. Realistically, we are all fallible human beings—things don't always go the way we would like. In fact, seldom if ever do things go perfectly! That doesn't mean we cannot enjoy sex very much even when it is not perfect.

5. *The sexes are completely different.* These beliefs are that "men and women are mysteriously different from each other" and that "men and women will never really understand each other." Such beliefs discourage us from trying to understand and appreciate our spouse and inhibit our adapting to each other's differences. It also discourages appreciating our many similarities.

If, by contrast, you believe that the sexes are more alike than different (which is what research shows),[6] you will likely also believe that "we can work it out because both of us have similar needs." This belief encourages you to be optimistic and leads to discussions with your spouse that are productive.

✥ Traits That Contribute to Marital Satisfaction

Just as several personality traits and attitudes may inhibit marital satisfaction, several may contribute to it, including these:

- Sociability
- Flexibility
- Good self-esteem
- Assertiveness
- Love
- Commitment

Sociability is often referred to as extroversion. Extroverts are sociable—they feel comfortable in the presence of others and talking to others openly about their thoughts, feelings, and needs. Such individuals are more likely to have satisfying marriages. This is because marriage is an intimate relationship where people expect to talk on an intimate level. They also expect their partner to openly and directly communicate what they want and need in an honest way. This is referred to as assertiveness. Linda (thirty-eight) described her husband Peter (forty) like this: "With Peter, I usually know what he wants and where I stand. I don't have to guess what he's thinking or feeling. That makes life much easier because it's not a guessing game." In other words, he's assertive.

Joe (twenty-five) described Becky (twenty-six) this way: "She's really open with her opinions and likes and dislikes. She's not a mystery woman at all. I like that—we have few misunderstandings."

My wife recently embroidered and framed a motto that emphasizes another important trait she and I have that has made our marriage work: flexibility. Flexibility is important because of the myriad unforeseen changes, unexpected events, and miscalculations we make in life. Flexible individuals roll with the punches. In contrast, rigid individuals struggle with changes. A change can mess up their whole day. This makes them irritable and hence frustrating to live with. Flexibility is a basic life skill that we all must learn to survive in a complex world and a busy marriage. It's probably obvious to you why self-esteem is important in marriage. Without good esteem and a good self-image, it is very difficult to be a full-functioning spouse. Such individuals stand up for themselves in a disagreement, speak their mind in a decision-making session with their partner, fulfill their spousal and parental responsibilities, and communicate better.

⚘ Two Especially Vital Traits

The last two positive predictors relate to your feelings and attitudes about your partner: love and commitment. They are vital to marital satisfaction.

Love

Just how much do you love your partner? I'm referring to mature, companionate, friendship love. This is love that is caring and respectful of the other. It also includes emotional attachment. How emotionally connected are you? How deep is your devotion?

One of the most common complaints I hear in marital therapy is "I don't love him anymore." What she really means is, "We've lost that loving feeling." What is that loving feeling? Usually romantic love. Little do people realize that romantic love can be rekindled with some effort. But more important, are you best friends? How much do you care about his welfare? Are you attached to the point that you miss her when she's out of town for a few days?

The most important points to remember about love in marriage are these:

1. It's basic to the survival of the relationship.

2. We all expect to have it.

3. When we don't have it, we are very distressed.

4. Most of us don't know how to rekindle romantic love or nourish companionate love.

5. There are proven ways to rekindle and nourish both kinds of love.

6. You get out of something what you put into it—you have to express love to get love.

The "investment of time and energy in our spouses helps us feel commitment and love in our marriage. Love flows more freely from what we give than what we get from others—the more we put in, the more we get out."[7] (More resources on how to improve love in your marriage are given in Chapter Seven.)

Commitment

How committed are you to your spouse as your partner for life? How committed are you to the institution of marriage? That is, do you believe that marriage is better than singlehood and should be a once-only, permanent relationship that is valued, protected, and nourished? Commitment is like glue in marriage. If it's a strong glue, it keeps you together through the expected (such as child bearing) and unexpected (such as job loss) events of married life. It keeps you true to your partner. It helps you keep trying when things are especially difficult. It helps you forgive her. It helps you remember him. It keeps you going.

Nancy (forty) and Lance (forty-five) showed their commitment in this comment to me: "In difficult times we always remember our marriage vows. We also remember a saying from a book we read on the expected stresses in marriage: 'If marriage wasn't supposed to be hard at times, there would be no need for such strong marriage vows at the altar.'"

Now let's look at your scores on the short tests and interpret their meanings.

🕊 Scoring and Interpretation Guidelines

The short tests you took were brief measures of personality traits that predict marital satisfaction and dissatisfaction. Look back at Worksheet 3.1 for your responses on these short tests. Take the sum scores for each short test and enter them in the spaces provided in Worksheet 3.2.

Let's look first at your perceptions of your personality traits that are predictors of marital dissatisfaction. These are your liabilities or areas that need improvement. Compare your scores with the norm scores on the following tests:

- Anxiety

- Anger and hostility

- Depression

- Impulsivity

- Vulnerability to stress

Norm scores refer to the average scores for over two thousand married individuals aged eighteen through sixty-five who have completed these short tests from the RELATE instrument over the past few years. By comparing your scores to these norm scores, you will better understand how similar or different you are from others.

If your scores on any of these scales is 2 points or more above the norm scores, your score is considered high. This means you are significantly more anxious, angry, depressed, impulsive, or vulnerable to stress than the average married person in our sample. If your scores are at or below the norm scores, you are average or below average on these traits. That's good! Most individuals will have some high scores but mostly average or below-average scores on these traits. Now the good news: with good self-help resources, support from your loved ones, and in some cases therapy, you can overcome problems represented by high scores on these traits. However, if left untreated, they will inhibit your ability to have a satisfying marriage.

Trait	Range of Scores	Norm Score	Your Score
Extroversion (items 1–4)	4–20	13	_____
Anxiety (items 5–8)	4–20	11	_____
Flexibility (items 9–12)	4–20	16	_____
Anger and hostility (items 13–15)	3–15	8	_____
Depression (items 16–18)	3–15	8	_____
Impulsivity (items 19–21)	3–15	9	_____
Vulnerability to stress (items 22–24)	3–15	9	_____
Assertiveness (items 25–28)	4–20	11	_____
Self-esteem (items 29–32)	4–20	17	_____
Love (items 33–35)	3–15	12	_____
Commitment (items 36–38)	3–15	11	_____

Worksheet 3.2. Personality Traits Summary (Items 1–38).

Please note that the short tests used in this book should not be considered comprehensive evaluations of these personality traits. If, as a result of taking these short tests, you are concerned that you may be seriously depressed, impulsive, angry, or whatever, consult with a professional therapist who can assist you with more detailed testing, a psychological interview, and a diagnosis, as necessary. High scores on the short tests in this book should be considered warning signs that should direct you to a more in-depth assessment of your problems and their solutions.

So how do your scores on these negative traits compare to the norms? Write down the traits on which you scored high and those on which you scored average or below average:

High scores: _____

_____

Average or below-average scores: _____

_____

Whew! The hardest part is over! Now let's look at the personality traits and attitudes that predict marital satisfaction. These are strengths or assets for your marriage:

- Sociability

- Flexibility

- Assertiveness

- High self-esteem

Two other characteristics are not personality traits but important attitudes:

- Love
- Commitment

Compare your scores with the norm scores. If your scores on any of these short tests are 2 points or more *lower* than the norm scores, your scores are considered low. If your scores are at or higher than the norm scores, they are considered average or above average. Higher scores reflect more positive traits and attitudes related to marital satisfaction.

So what are your highest scores? A score reflects an asset or strength if it is at or above the norm score. Liabilities are represented by traits where you scored low. What traits need improvement? Write your responses here:

Low scores: _____

_____

🕸 Guidelines for Improving Personality Traits and Attitudes

If you scored higher than average on the negative traits that predict marital dissatisfaction, be assured that help is available! The first step in solving these problems is personal awareness. You have that now. The next step, as mentioned earlier, is further assessment. A professional therapist can help here. Guidelines on how to find a qualified therapist are presented in Chapter Seven. Research has shown that self-help books and programs can help many individuals overcome depression and anxiety.[8] These may be inexpensive and good starting points for you to pursue. (See my recommended books in Chapter Seven.) However, the more depressed and anxious you are, the more likely you will benefit from professional therapy or medications designed to reduce depression and anxiety (or both). The same applies for treating anger, impulsivity, and vulnerability to stress. It should be added that each of these problems (with perhaps the exception of impulsivity) may also have biological causes, so do not rule out seeing your family physician first if you are exhibiting significant symptoms.

Let me share an example of how this works. A couple I saw in marital therapy complained of frequent bickering and hostile feelings toward each other. He explained that she was a perfectionist. She complained that she seldom slept well and that no one ever helped her around the house. In our sessions, the wife was especially negative and hostile toward her husband. She was clearly depressed, anxious, and angry.

I had her complete a detailed depression inventory that indicated a clinical level of depression and anxiety. Upon my advice, she saw her physician, who prescribed an antidepressant medication, and she started individual therapy with me to overcome perfectionism. We also continued marital therapy. The individual and marital therapy got easier and more positive as the medication began to help her feel better.

Feeling better made her less vulnerable to stress. She became more patient with her husband. She started seeing his attempts to help her with housework that she overlooked when she was depressed. As her attitude and mood improved, he was more willing to be helpful and loving toward her. Criticism waned as progress was made in resolving their problems. However, without the prerequisite improvement in her mood, they would still be in marriage counseling but not making much progress.

Now let's turn to positive personality traits. How high were your scores on the following positive traits and attitudes?

- Sociability or extroversion
- Flexibility
- Assertion
- Self-esteem
- Love
- Commitment

If your scores were average or high, congratulations! If not, don't worry—these traits can be enhanced just as negative traits can be overcome. Excellent self-help programs are available to increase your sociability or comfort in conversing with people, self-esteem, flexibility, and assertiveness. (Recommended self-help books are presented in Chapter Seven.) By becoming more comfortable in conversations with your partner, you will become better acquainted and better able to fulfill each other's needs.

Assertiveness refers to comfort in speaking up and telling people what you want and need in a respectful but clear manner. Your partner cannot read your mind! She needs to know what you are thinking and feeling on a topic and, most important, what you want or need.

Flexibility can be learned, too. The more flexible you are, the less vulnerable you are to stress and the more willing you will be to compromise with your spouse when necessary. The opposite trait—rigidly—causes problems that are usually referred to as "stubbornness" or "pigheadedness." These terms suggest an unwillingness to look at your partner's position with empathy or to consider compromise, change your mind, reconsider, or meet her halfway. Rigidity usually shows up in decision making and creates a power struggle. Many times these power struggles have no end and result in impasses, resentment, and hurt feelings. What you need to understand is that rigidity is a *choice*. Flexibility is, too. You can learn to be more flexible. You may have to face some fears (for example, losing control or power). You may have to seek professional therapy to become less rigid. But with a sincere commitment to change and the right help, you can do it!

⚘ Two Key Attitudes for Marital Satisfaction

Love and commitment are two key attitudes that cause marriage to bloom. How did you score on these two attitudes? If you scored low, can anything be done? Fortunately, yes. Let's take love first.

Loving Your Spouse Again

A forty-five-year-old wife told me in therapy that she was not sure she loved her husband anymore. She felt little attachment or love. It seemed that their love had wilted over the years amid all the distractions of careers, raising kids, managing a home and budget, and so on. She had indeed "lost that loving feeling." When she asked, "Can I ever get it back?" I answered, "If you try."

Here are some guidelines for loving your spouse again.

1. *Think about a time in the past when you did love him.* How were things different then? My guess is that you were less stressed, you spent more time together, you enjoyed mutual activities, and you did more favors for each other. You can rekindle love by thinking back on how you used to show love to each other. There lie keys for today. Although you're different today and circumstances have changed, you can still revive behaviors, attitudes, and rituals that worked for you before (for example, arrange a date alone every week).

2. *Give love to get love.* It's required. And it starts with you! You don't have to wait for your partner. Instead, take the high road, regardless of where your spouse is along the way. The investment of time and energy in your spouse will help you feel more love and commitment.[9] In what ways have you been showing or giving love to your spouse lately?

3. Set goals to improve the love in your marriage by increasing nourishing behaviors and avoiding destructive behaviors (see Exhibit 3.1).

Behaviors That Nourish Love	Behaviors That Destroy Love
Sharing feelings regularly	Negligence
Thoughtfulness (for example, a surprise flower or card)	Criticism, nagging
	Pointing out inadequacies
Compliments	Ignoring your partner
Shared activities both of you enjoy	Placing a low priority on your partner
Sacrificing for each other	Unresolved conflict
Service to each other	Defensiveness
Kind words	Forgetting your partner's birthday or your anniversary
Empathy	
Prioritizing your marriage	Neglecting your looks and personal fitness
Accepting your partner's faults	Selfishness
Looking your best	Disrespect
Respect	

Exhibit 3.1. Effects of Various Behaviors on Love.

Regaining Commitment

Commitment keeps you together in times of stress or crisis and during challenges to your marriage (such as taking a job requiring travel out of town frequently). Commitment begins before your wedding day. When you marry, you pledge yourself and your fidelity at the altar. Then the hard work begins! As mentioned earlier, if marriage were not a stressful relationship, why would we need to exchange such strong marriage vows?

I like Stanley and Markman's definition of *commitment* as "personal dedication."[10] This refers to your decision to maintain or improve the quality of your marriage for the joint benefit of yourself and your spouse. It involves sacrificing for it, investing in it, linking your personal goals to it, and considering your partner's welfare, not solely your own. Here's an example of high commitment: Keith (thirty-one) showed Sara (thirty-two) commitment when he was offered a better-paying position two thousand miles away. Their marriage was young, and Sara had just started graduate school where they were living. Keith considered Sara's feelings and educational goals before making his decision (he considered her welfare). Could she attend an equally good graduate program in the new location if they transferred (linking the personal goals of career satisfaction for both spouses)? Ultimately, he turned down the offer (he sacrificed). *Constraint commitment* is another form of commitment that stems from constraints on ending a marriage, such as economic loss, embarrassment, or psychological costs such as a sense of failure or guilt. To me this is a "second-class" form of commitment that is usually instigated only by chronically unsatisfied and divorce-prone couples.

So how committed are you to your spouse? You can always increase your commitment. Add love to commitment, and you can overcome just about any marital problems.

🕉 Emotional Problems and Physical Health

How did you answer items 39 and 40 on Worksheet 3.1? If you answered "Yes" or "Unsure" to these items, what is stopping you from seeking treatment by a qualified professional? How is the problem affecting your marital satisfaction? Is denial that you have a problem the real problem? Or is it embarrassment to admit a problem? Or perhaps pride is getting in the way of your solving the problem.

It takes a strong person to seek therapy or medical attention for her problems. Are you that strong? Or do you simply not know where to seek help? A good place to get referrals for therapy or medical help is from a trusted relative or friend who has successfully overcome a similar problem himself. That is, consumers are the best referral sources. A second source is your clergyperson, who knows the best resources in your community. In Chapter Seven, I include directions for finding a competent therapist and questions to ask a therapist before your first session.

🕸 Dysfunctional Beliefs That Hinder Marital Satisfaction

Now let's look at your responses to items that measure dysfunctional beliefs. Check your scores on items 41–43. They measure your belief that disagreement in marriage is bad. A high score on this scale is 7 or higher. Disagreements in marriage do not have to be destructive—in fact, for most couples they usually are not. It depends on how you handle disagreements. If you do so by listening respectfully, avoiding criticism and defensiveness, and compromising when necessary, disagreements can actually strengthen a marriage by helping partners understand each other better and feel pride when a disagreement is successfully resolved.

In addition, when couples tell me they have never disagreed, it usually means one of the following things:[11]

They have only known each other for a week.

They are in denial.

They are conflict-phobic.

They never discuss meaningful topics.

One person is submissive enough to just shut up when disagreements arise.

They have given up trying to resolve their differences and are hence living in a state of frustration and quiet resentment.

They are lying to save face.

Their goal is to get into the *Guinness Book of World Records* as the only couple on earth never to have an argument!

If your score is high on this short test of "disagreement is always bad," reconsider your belief. Perhaps you believe that heated conflicts rather than simple disagreements are bad. Conflict often denotes hot, angry, or out-of-control fights. Is this the case for you? Also, ask yourself these questions: What is my logic behind this belief? Does it make sense to others when I explain it to them? What evidence do I have that supports this belief? For example, what have I seen or heard that supports this belief?

Have I observed situations where this belief was challenged? For example, have you ever seen a couple disagree successfully? How did it affect their relationship for the better? When have you seen a couple rigidly avoid disagreements and the relationship suffered?

You needn't rely on your own internal resources and observations. Read good books about how to resolve disagreements successfully in marriage. (See Chapter Seven for several suggestions.) Interview a couple who resolve disagreements successfully and are happily married. How do they do it? What did you learn from them that you can apply in your marriage?

If your score on this short test of disagreements was at or below the norm score, great! This dysfunctional belief will probably not hinder your resolution of disagreements or damage your marital satisfaction.

Now check your score on items 44–46. A high score (9 or above) means that you probably believe in ESP, that is, you think people can read each other's minds. If true, this would make communication in marriage unnecessary most of the time. However, there is no scientific evidence for ESP in marriage, even though spouses may become progressively better at guessing what their partner is thinking or wants on occasion. So speak up about what you think, feel, and want! To challenge your belief in this myth, use the same challenging techniques described earlier for the disagreement belief. If you do not hold the ESP belief, you will be more likely to get your needs met and fulfill your partner's needs. There will also be fewer misunderstandings.

Adjusting for Differences

Your score on items 47–49 indicates how much you believe that your partner cannot change. A score of 9 or more is high. Such a negative view of your partner will result in much frustration and discouragement for both of you. Hope and trust will erode. The truth is, if people couldn't change, there would be no need for the many thousands of therapists and psychiatrists in the world who help millions of people change their lives every day. Change may sometimes be difficult or occur slowly, but it is a frequent and common phenomenon. Coping with the normal stresses of marriage and life requires changes in you and your partner. So don't hang on to a negative, unrealistic, and constraining belief in changelessness. Ask yourself challenging questions similar to those for the disagreement belief, and you can arrive at a more realistic understanding, such as "People often change for the better—it's a fortunate part of life and relationships."

What is your score for the items 50–52? A high score is 9 or more. A high score reflects a "sexual perfectionism" belief. You expect yourself and your partner to perform well under any and all circumstances. Of course, that is not humanly possible. All of us get tired, stressed out, preoccupied, and so on, and these emotional or physical conditions make it unlikely that we or our partners can perform sexually as we would like every single time. So give yourselves a break! Ours is an imperfect world, filled with imperfect people and relationships. Don't expect perfection in your sexual relationship or any other part of your marriage.

Finally, what is your score on the "sexes are different" scale (items 53–55)? A high score is 9 or more. If you hold this constraining belief, you will fail to solve many marital problems. You may give up even trying to understand your partner. You will take the easy way out and blame a lack of solutions to problems on unsubstantiated sex differences rather than a lack of serious effort or skills to resolve differences or understand each other. Fortunately, as noted earlier, men and women are more alike than different overall. And today we understand these differences better, know how to adjust to them, and in many cases make the differences serve as strengths in a marriage.[12] If your score on these items was relatively low, your belief that men and women can understand each other and that differences are mostly learned rather than innate will be a resource for you in marriage.

If your score was high, perhaps you just lack scientific information on sex differences. If so, I recommended reading research-based self-help books on the topic of sex differences in marriage, such as *Fighting for Your Marriage*.[13] Be cautious when reading other books based strictly on the author's personal or clinical experiences or observations.

✿ Your Big Picture

In summary, what does the big picture look like? That is, what are your strengths and weaknesses in the area of individual traits related to marital satisfaction as outlined in this chapter? List them here:

Assets   *Liabilities*

_____   _____

_____   _____

_____   _____

_____   _____

_____   _____

_____   _____

_____   _____

_____   _____

What is your ratio of strengths to liabilities? Overall, are your individual traits mostly a strength or a liability for you? What does this mean to you? What can you do now to strengthen your individual traits identified in this chapter? Who can help you do this? When will you begin?

_____

_____

_____

_____

_____

Congratulations on your strengths, and best of luck working to improve yourself.

We have now assessed one factor in the Marriage Triangle—your individual traits. In the next chapter you will learn about and assess couple traits related to marital satisfaction and dissatisfaction. Continue to be open-minded and honest in answering the questionnaires and discussing the results with your partner.

The Great Marriage Tune-Up Book

Factor 2

Your Couple Traits

Jackson always tells me what's on his mind. More than that, he tells me what's in his heart, too, in a way that does not offend me.

—Dawn, thirty-one-year-old respiratory therapist

I can depend on Lilly to listen to what's on my mind—she never interrupts me or tries to solve anything. That helps my self-confidence.

—Lee, forty-two-year-old insurance adjuster

Our sex life is not perfect, but we really enjoy each other when we get the time. Those times really bond us.

—Carma, twenty-eight-year-old teacher

We see eye-to-eye on most things. I'm sure glad because I see other couples frequently squabbling over big differences of opinion on important matters.

—Tyson, forty-five-year-old engineer

These comments reflect some of the important couple predictors of marital satisfaction—good communication skills, sexual satisfaction, and consensus on important matters in marriage such as time spent together, how decisions are made, and marital roles. The purpose of this chapter is to explain the couple traits that are the most important predictors of your marital satisfaction, including these:

- Couple communication skills (speaking and listening skills)
- Conflict resolution skills
- Degree of intimacy, including affection and sexual enjoyment
- Degree of consensus or agreement on life's major issues (such as finances and raising children)
- Degree of cohesion, including time together and emotional closeness
- Fair sharing of power

A second purpose of this chapter is to explain several negative interaction styles that predict dissatisfaction in marriage—these are communication behaviors you should avoid:[1]

- Criticism
- Defensiveness
- Contempt (attacking your partner's personality)
- Stonewalling (withdrawing emotionally in stony silence when your spouse offends you)

In this chapter you will also assess your overall satisfaction with your marriage and compare your scores to national norms.

In Chapter Three I referred to individual traits as being like the nucleus of a cell, as shown in Figure 2.2. Couple traits are just as important as individual traits. In the couple realm, interaction takes place between the two parts of the nucleus—messages are sent, information is received, problems are solved, and so on. The quality of that interaction or communication is perhaps the *single most important predictor* of marital satisfaction.

Communication is the heart of a marriage—it determines how well the rest of the marriage functions. That is, with good communication skills, individual problems can be overcome, stresses dealt with in a healthy and efficient manner, disagreements resolved to both spouses' satisfaction, love expressed, and other matters discussed frankly and objectively.

Let's look at an example of how the couple traits on our list intersect to either increase or decrease your marital satisfaction. Jane (thirty-six) and Hugh (thirty-seven) had been married twelve years when they saw me for marital therapy. The first part of counseling was spent assessing their Marriage Triangle as shown in this book. When we analyzed the results, I discovered that Jane was very talkative and liked to jump in and solve marital problems "right now!" In their conversations, she would often interrupt or speak for Hugh (saying things like, "I know you really agree with me") before he had a chance to reply. She showed little ability to listen. Hugh struggled to express his thoughts, feelings, or wants to her. Their conflict resolution sessions in my office went nowhere—they could not even stay on the topic at hand. Furthermore, the rest of their couple realm showed additional flaws:

- Lack of consensus on how to deal with in-laws, frequency of sex, and demonstrations of affection
- Too little time spent together in mutually fulfilling activities
- No feelings of emotional closeness

Their poor communication skills handicapped them and prevented them from resolving these other marital issues. Therefore, much of our time together was spent first learning how to speak and listen to each other respectfully. Only then were they prepared to resolve their differences, plan recreation together, and become emotionally closer.

Before going any further, let's do an assessment of your key couple traits. We will start with a behavioral assessment of your communication skills on Worksheet 4.1. You will then complete further short tests using Worksheet 4.2.

To get the most out of this book, make sure you've completed these assessments of your couple traits before reading further. At the end of this chapter, I will instruct you on what your scores mean and how to use them to improve your marriage. Since communication and conflict resolution skills are more objectively measured by observation rather than self-reporting, I would like you to examine your communication skills first by completing an informative exercise called the Couple Communication Assessment.

Couple Communication Assessment Exercise

This exercise will help you identify your positive and negative couple communication skills and styles.[2] First, prepare a cassette deck ahead of time so you can record the conversation you will have. Be sure to first test the volume control on record mode so that you can hear everyone clearly during the playback. Sit together in a quiet place where you will not be interrupted. Set the recorder between you to get the best recording while talking. Now decide on a topic or issue on which the two of you disagree. Examples might be vacation choices, in-laws, career plans, how many children to have, birth control, budgeting money, or anything else that you genuinely care about. (Please don't have a fight while trying to decide!) Turn on the recorder, and begin discussing the topic. Continue the discussion for about three minutes. Then stop the recording.

To score this behavioral measure of your communication and conflict resolution skills, first rewind the tape to the beginning of your conversation. Each of you should score yourself, not your partner, on each of the communication behaviors listed on Worksheet 4.1. As you play the tape, stop after each short segment of interaction and score your skills. This will require that you listen to small segments of the tape at a time until you have listened to the entire conversation. Don't feel overwhelmed! This is only a three-minute interaction. Even though it is a short conversation, you will learn much about your communication and conflict resolution skills.

Next, complete Worksheet 4.2, which deals with your communication and conflict resolution skills.

As promised earlier, at the end of the chapter I will show you how to use your scores and responses on these worksheets to determine your strengths and areas for improvement in your couple realm. But first let's look carefully at the relationship between these couple traits and marital satisfaction.

✸ The Importance of Communication

Good communication is the "oil in the marriage engine." That is, none of the marriage parts will work smoothly if good communication and conflict resolution are missing. Good communication involves two factors: (1) a loving and cooperative attitude toward your partner and (2) good communication skills.

Without a loving attitude, you might as well not worry about your skills! Partners with a selfish attitude but good skills are only good manipulators. Their responses to their partner often sounds like this: "I can see how important this is to you, but I still say we're going to do it my way."

Your attitude is up to you—I cannot help you much with that except to sensitize you to the importance of it when having an important discussion with your spouse.

Mark how many times during your three-minute conversation each of you did each of the following:

	Her	Him

Positive Speaking Skills

1. I expressed a thought, feeling, or intention in a respectful way. _____ _____

2. I made positive suggestions to resolve our disagreement. _____ _____

Add up the number of times each of you used each of the positive speaking skills in items 1 and 2, and write your totals here: _____ _____

Negative Speaking Skills

3. I kept my thoughts, feelings, or intentions to myself and said little. _____ _____

4. I made no suggestion or negative suggestions to resolve our disagreement. _____ _____

5. I tried to force my solution to the problem on my partner. _____ _____

Add up the number of times each of you used each of the negative speaking skills in items 3–5, and write your totals here: _____ _____

Positive Listening Skills

6. I asked my partner for his or her opinion. _____ _____

7. I responded to my partner's comments or solutions to the problem in a tolerant, caring way. _____ _____

Add up the number of times each of you used each of the positive listening skills in items 6 and 7, and write your totals here: _____ _____

Negative Listening Skills

8. I was intolerant or judgmental about my partner's point of view. _____ _____

9. I interrupted my partner when he or she was speaking. _____ _____

Add up the number of times each of you used each of the negative listening skills in items 8 and 9, and write your totals here: _____ _____

Worksheet 4.1. Scoring Sheet for Couple Communication Assessment Exercise.[3]

Nonverbal Behaviors

The next group of items asks each of you to rate your nonverbal behaviors during the interaction. (For these items, you will have to rely on your memory rather than the audiotape.) Read each item, and respond using the rating scale to the right of each item. Mark an X over the number for his response, and circle the number for her response.

Circle Your Responses:

	Strongly Disagree	Disagree	Undecided	Agree	Strongly Agree

Positive Behaviors

	Strongly Disagree	Disagree	Undecided	Agree	Strongly Agree
10. I maintained direct eye contact.	1	2	3	4	5
11. I nodded my head or said "uh huh" occasionally to show my partner I was listening.	1	2	3	4	5

Negative Behaviors

	Strongly Disagree	Disagree	Undecided	Agree	Strongly Agree
12. I slouched back in my chair most of the time while listening.	1	2	3	4	5
13. My arms or legs were crossed most of the time.	1	2	3	4	5

The next group of items asks each of you to rate the overall conversation. Read each item, and respond by using the rating scale to the right of each item. Mark an X over the number for his response, and circle the number for her response.

14. This conversation helped our relationship.	1	2	3	4	5
15. We stayed with one issue and did not stray to other issues.	1	2	3	4	5
16. Each of us had about equal speaking time.	1	2	3	4	5

Worksheet 4.1. Scoring Sheet for Couple Communication Assessment Exercise. *Continued*

	Strongly Disagree	Disagree	Undecided	Agree	Strongly Agree

Circle Your Responses:

Empathic Communication

1. In most matters, I understand what my partner is saying.   1   2   3   4   5

2. I understand my partner's feelings.   1   2   3   4   5

3. I am able to listen to my partner in an understanding way.   1   2   3   4   5

Sum your responses to items 1–3, and write your score here: _____

Clear Sending

4. When I talk to my partner, I can say what I want in a clear manner.   1   2   3   4   5

5. I struggle to find words to express myself to my partner.   1   2   3   4   5

6. I discuss my personal problems with my partner.   1   2   3   4   5

First, reverse the score for item 5: if you circled 1, score it as 5; if you circled 2, score it as 4; 3 remains the same. Then sum your responses to items 4–6, and write your score here: _____

Partner's Empathic Communication

7. In most matters, my partner understands what I'm trying to say.   1   2   3   4   5

8. My partner understands my feelings.   1   2   3   4   5

9. My partner is able to listen to me in an understanding way.   1   2   3   4   5

Sum your responses to items 7–9, and write your score here: _____

Worksheet 4.2. Assessing Couple Traits: Communication and Conflict Resolution Skills.[4]

	Strongly Disagree	Disagree	Undecided	Agree	Strongly Agree

Partner's Clear Sending

10. My partner can say what he or she wants to say in a clear manner. | 1 | 2 | 3 | 4 | 5

11. My partner struggles to find words to express himself or herself. | 1 | 2 | 3 | 4 | 5

12. My partner discusses his or her personal problems with me. | 1 | 2 | 3 | 4 | 5

Reverse-score item 11; then sum your responses to items 10–12, and write your score here: _____

Conflict Resolution Responses

The following items refer to how you and your spouse resolve problems or conflict in your relationship.

Circle Your Responses:

	Never	Seldom	Sometimes	Frequently	Always

Exit Responses

13. When I'm unhappy with my partner, I consider breaking up. | 1 | 2 | 3 | 4 | 5

14. When I'm irritated with my partner, I think about ending our relationship. | 1 | 2 | 3 | 4 | 5

15. When I'm dissatisfied with our relationship, I consider initiating a relationship with someone else. | 1 | 2 | 3 | 4 | 5

Sum your responses to items 13–15, and write your score here: _____

Worksheet 4.2. Assessing Couple Traits: Communication and Conflict Resolution Skills, *Continued*

	Never	Seldom	Sometimes	Frequently	Always

Voice Responses

16. When my partner says or does things I don't like, I talk to him or her about what's upsetting me.   1   2   3   4   5

17. When things aren't going well between us, I suggest changing things in the relationship in order to solve the problem.   1   2   3   4   5

18. When my partner and I are angry with one another, I suggest a compromise.   1   2   3   4   5

Sum your responses to items 16–18, and write your score here: _____

Loyalty Responses

19. When we have problems in our relationship, I patiently wait for things to improve.   1   2   3   4   5

20. When there are things about my partner that I don't like, I accept his or her faults and weaknesses and don't try to change him or her.   1   2   3   4   5

21. When my partner is inconsiderate, I give him or her the benefit of the doubt and forget about it.   1   2   3   4   5

Sum your responses to items 19–21, and write your score here: _____

Neglect Responses

22. When my partner and I have problems, I refuse to talk to him or her about it.   1   2   3   4   5

Worksheet 4.2. Assessing Couple Traits: Communication and Conflict Resolution Skills, *Continued*

	Circle Your Responses:				
	Never	*Seldom*	*Sometimes*	*Frequently*	*Always*
23. When I'm really bothered about something my partner has done, I criticize him or her for things that are unrelated to the real problem.	1	2	3	4	5
24. When I'm upset with my partner, I ignore him or her for a while.	1	2	3	4	5

Sum your responses to items 22–24, and write your score here: _____

Negative Interaction Styles

The following traits refer to negative interaction styles in your marriage.

	Circle Your Responses:				
	Strongly Disagree	*Disagree*	*Undecided*	*Agree*	*Strongly Agree*
Criticism					
25. I don't censor my complaints at all. I really let my partner have them full force.	1	2	3	4	5
26. I use a tactless choice of words when I complain.	1	2	3	4	5
27. There's no stopping me once I get started complaining.	1	2	3	4	5

Sum your responses to items 25–27, and write your score here: _____

Contempt and Defensiveness

28. I have no respect for my partner when we are discussing an issue.	1	2	3	4	5

Worksheet 4.2. Assessing Couple Traits: Communication and Conflict Resolution Skills, *Continued*

	Circle Your Responses:				
	Strongly Disagree	*Disagree*	*Undecided*	*Agree*	*Strongly Agree*
29. When I get upset, I can see glaring faults in my partner's personality.	1	2	3	4	5
30. When my partner complains, I feel that I have to "ward off" these attacks.	1	2	3	4	5
31. I feel unfairly attacked when my partner is being negative.	1	2	3	4	5

Sum your responses to items 28–31, and write your score here: _____

Stonewalling

32. In a conflict, I think, "It's best to withdraw to avoid a big fight."	1	2	3	4	5
33. In a conflict, I think that withdrawing is the best solution.	1	2	3	4	5
34. In a conflict, I don't want to fan the flames of conflict, so I just sit back and wait.	1	2	3	4	5
35. In a conflict, I withdraw to try to calm down.	1	2	3	4	5

Sum your responses to items 32–35, and write your score here: _____

Flooding in Conflict Management

36. Whenever I have a conflict with my partner, I feel physically tense and anxious, and I don't think clearly.	1	2	3	4	5
37. I feel physically tired or drained after I have a conflict with my partner.	1	2	3	4	5
38. Whenever we have a conflict, the feelings I have are overwhelming.	1	2	3	4	5

Sum your responses to items 36–38, and write your score here: _____

Worksheet 4.2. Assessing Couple Traits: Communication and Conflict Resolution Skills, *Continued*

	Strongly Disagree	Disagree	Undecided	Agree	Strongly Agree

Soothing in Conflict Management

39. When I am in an argument, I recognize when I am overwhelmed and then make a deliberate effort to calm myself down.   1   2   3   4   5

40. While in an argument, I recognize when my partner is overwhelmed and then make a deliberate effort to calm him or her down.   1   2   3   4   5

41. I've found that during an intense argument, it is better to take a break, calm down, and then return to discuss the matter later.   1   2   3   4   5

Sum your responses to items 39–41, and write your score here: _____

Intimacy: Affection

42. I often kiss my spouse good-bye.   1   2   3   4   5

43. I often tell my spouse, "I love you."   1   2   3   4   5

44. Buying gifts shows my affection for my spouse.   1   2   3   4   5

Sum your responses to items 42–44, and write your score here: _____

Intimacy: Sex

45. I feel that our sex life is lacking in quality.   1   2   3   4   5

46. I feel that our sex life really adds a lot to our relationship.   1   2   3   4   5

47. I feel that our sex life is boring.   1   2   3   4   5

Reverse-score items 45 and 47. Then sum your responses to items 45–47, and write your score here: _____

Worksheet 4.2. Assessing Couple Traits: Communication and Conflict Resolution Skills, *Continued*

	Always	*Almost Always*	*Frequently*	*Occasionally*	*Almost Always*	*Always*

Consensus

Most people have disagreements in their relationships. Indicate the approximate extent of agreement or disagreement between you and your partner for each item.

	Disagree				*Agree*	
48. Religious matters	0	1	2	3	4	5
49. Demonstrations of affection	0	1	2	3	4	5
50. Making major decisions	0	1	2	3	4	5
51. Sex relations	0	1	2	3	4	5
52. Conventionality (correct or proper behavior)	0	1	2	3	4	5
53. Career decisions	0	1	2	3	4	5

Sum your responses to items 48–53, and write your score here: _____

Cohesion: Closeness

Circle Your Responses:

	Almost Never	*Once in a While*	*Sometimes*	*Frequently*	*Always*
54. We are supportive of each other during difficult times.	1	2	3	4	5
55. It is easier to discuss problems with people outside our marriage than with each other.	1	2	3	4	5

Worksheet 4.2. Assessing Couple Traits: Communication and Conflict Resolution Skills, *Continued*

	Almost Never	Once in a While	Sometimes	Frequently	Always
56. We feel very close to each other.	1	2	3	4	5

Reverse-score item 55; then sum your responses to items 54–56, and write your score here: _____

Cohesion: Togetherness

	Strongly Disagree	Disagree	Undecided	Agree	Strongly Agree
57. In our marriage, having time alone is more important than togetherness.	1	2	3	4	5
58. A husband and wife do not need to share many of the same recreational interests or hobbies with each other.	1	2	3	4	5
59. It is important for a husband and wife to have many of the same friends and to like each other's friends.	1	2	3	4	5

Reverse-score items 57 and 58; then sum your responses to items 57–59, and write your score here: _____

Worksheet 4.2. Assessing Couple Traits: Communication and Conflict Resolution Skills, *Continued*

Overall Marital Satisfaction

These items assess your overall marital satisfaction, taking all of the preceding factors into consideration.

Circle Your Responses:

	Extremely	Very	Somewhat		Somewhat	Very	Extremely
	Dissatisfied			*Mixed Feelings*		*Satisfied*	
60. How satisfied are you with your marriage?	1	2	3	4	5	6	7
61. How satisfied are you with your husband or wife as a spouse?	1	2	3	4	5	6	7
62. How satisfied are you with your relationship with your spouse?	1	2	3	4	5	6	7

Sum your responses to items 60–62, and write your score here: _____

Conventionality

These items measure your overall attitude about marriage and your spouse.

Circle Your Responses:

	Strongly Disagree	Disagree	Undecided	Agree	Strongly Agree
63. My partner has all the qualities I've ever wanted in a mate.	1	2	3	4	5
64. My partner and I understand each other completely.	1	2	3	4	5
65. I have some needs that are not being met in my relationship.	1	2	3	4	5

Reverse-score item 65; then sum your responses to items 63–65, and write your score here: _____

Worksheet 4.2. Assessing Couple Traits: Communication and Conflict Resolution Skills, *Continued*

	Never	*Rarely*	*Sometimes*	*Often*	*Very Often*
					Circle Your Responses:

Problem Areas Checklist

How often have the following areas been a problem in your relationship?

	Never	*Rarely*	*Sometimes*	*Often*	*Very Often*
66. Financial matters	1	2	3	4	5
67. Having children	1	2	3	4	5
68. Rearing children	1	2	3	4	5
69. Parents and in-laws	1	2	3	4	5
70. Roles (who does what)	1	2	3	4	5
71. Weight	1	2	3	4	5
72. Who's in charge (power)	1	2	3	4	5
73. Substance abuse	1	2	3	4	5
74. Violence	1	2	3	4	5
75. Infidelity	1	2	3	4	5
76. Household management	1	2	3	4	5

Worksheet 4.2. Assessing Couple Traits: Communication and Conflict Resolution Skills, *Continued*

	Never	*Sometimes*	*Frequently*

More Serious Marital Problems

In some marriages, violence or alcohol or substance abuse occurs. The following items that measure the extent of these problems in your marriage.

	Never	Sometimes	Frequently
77. My partner or I push, slap, kick, hit, or throw objects at the other when upset.	1	2	3
78. My partner or I ridicule, insult, call names, or threaten the other when upset.	1	2	3
79. My partner or I force the other to do things he or she does not want to do, especially sexually.	1	2	3
80. My partner or I use alcohol or illegal drugs to the extent that it causes problems at work, at school, or in our relationship.	1	2	3
81. My partner or I have had legal problems (for example, a DUI arrest) as a result of using alcohol or illegal drugs.	1	2	3
82. My partner or I have tried unsuccessfully to stop using alcohol or illegal drugs.	1	2	3
83. My partner or I have had an affair.	Yes		No

Worksheet 4.2. Assessing Couple Traits: Communication and Conflict Resolution Skills, *Continued*

If your attitude is poor—perhaps not due to a personal weakness but rather as a result of fatigue, stress, or anger—take a relaxation break before talking to your partner. Make an attitude adjustment. When you feel you can approach her more calmly and lovingly, think about using these communication skills: effective speaking (sending) and empathic listening (receiving).

Effective Speaking

To be an effective speaker, you first need to clarify in your mind what you want to say about a topic.[5] What are you *thinking?* How do you *feel?* What do you *want?* An effective message might look something like the following:

1. "I was thinking about our plans this weekend, and I don't believe we can both go to the game and see your parents. That disappoints and frustrates me, but I don't think it will work. I want to do both; that is the problem."

2. "I want to sit down and discuss our budget because I think it's out of control. That disturbs me a lot!"

3. "I expected you to get that done. I thought you agreed yesterday that you would do it for me. Now that I've discovered that it's not done, it makes me mad. I want us to resolve this today, if possible."

Notice in each example that the person speaks for himself or herself. Using the pronoun *I* shows that you are taking ownership of the problem rather than blaming your partner. You also avoid frustrating your partner by not leaving out what you *want to do.* You and your partner will likely discover that at least one part of these three-part messages (what I think, what I feel, what I want) are a challenge for you to identify and express. For example, some people struggle to find an appropriate word for their feelings. Some struggle to say what they want. With practice, however, you can become skilled at expressing all three.

Using these simple guidelines will help you be more assertive with your partner without offending her. Just be careful not to add insults or blaming phrases to your message. For example, "I am frustrated that you were irresponsible again and picked me up late. I want you to act more like an adult and learn how to read a clock!" With these kinds of insults and blaming phrases, this formula will not work. Avoid insulting, blaming, or criticizing your partner.

Empathic Listening

This second skill is also called paraphrasing or reflecting. You are in fact acting like a mirror, reflecting in your own words what your partner has just said. The most important thing is to catch the feelings being expressed. You do this in a nonjudgmental way, without editing what was said by adding your own comments or opinion. This skill is called empathy—standing in your partner's shoes temporarily and seeing the world from her perspective. This kind of listening is not used in everyday conversation when we are making small talk ("How's the weather there?") or shop talk ("Who's going to fix dinner tonight?"). It's only used when your partner is expressing personal feelings, thoughts, and wants on an important topic. Here is how someone might use empathic listening in response to each of the three examples of effective speaking cited earlier:

1. "You're frustrated because you want to do both."
2. "You're really nervous about the budget."
3. "It's really important to you to resolve this problem now."

If you were the original effective speaker in our examples, how would you feel if your partner responded in these ways to your messages? Understood? Accepted? Valued? Notice that empathic listening does not include offering advice, acting irritated, or being defensive in responding (as in "Well, you should just do it yourself if you're in such a big hurry!") or ignoring your partner. Instead, just paraphrase in your own words how he feels and reflect it back to him. It works! After listening to him in this empathic way, you have earned the right to express your own thoughts, feelings, and wants or to ask him if he would like some advice. If he agrees, you can make suggestions. The problem is that most partners offer advice too early in the conversation, before they have earned the right (through empathic listening) to offer advice. Many times, advice is not only not wanted but not needed. People usually have already come up with their own solutions—they just needed to blow off some steam first.[6]

Related speaking and listening skills (speaking in a respectful way, listening for feelings) are discussed further as part of conflict resolution skills. Resolving conflict in a healthy way is one of the *single best predictors* of your marital satisfaction. Hence it is essential that you make an accurate assessment of your ability to do so.

❀ Conflict Resolution Skills

Effective conflict resolution first involves the use of effective speaking and empathic listening skills as just described. In addition, the following related skills help couples deal effectively with conflict and at the same time enrich their relationship.[7]

- Using respect when stating your opinion
- Making positive suggestions
- Avoiding forcing your solution on your partner
- Not straying from the topic at hand
- Calming yourself when the disagreement is intense
- Using a caring tone of voice
- Avoiding interrupting
- Asking your partner for his opinion
- Giving your partner equal speaking time
- Maintaining eye contact and an open body position (for example, not crossing your arms or fidgeting)
- Calming your partner when the disagreement is intense

A Conflict Successfully Managed

Here is an example of how a couple dealt with a conflict in a marital therapy session in my office. They had learned many of the skills described in this chapter, partly by observing their parents' good role modeling and partly as a result of participating in a marriage enhancement course at their church. The topic they discussed was how to deal with their stressful financial situation. Previous assessment indicated there was still disagreement or conflict about how to solve it.

DON: I think our finances are out of control. Every time I write a check, I worry that it may not clear the bank. So I always feel nervous—it's almost like a panic attack every time I open the checkbook. *(expressions of thoughts and feelings)*

LORA: You do stress out at even the sight of the checkbook! *(empathic response)*

DON: Yeah! It's like I don't even want to open the darn thing and face paying a bill! But I know bills must be paid. I just want a better system of accounting for our expenses. And I want us to do it together. *(expression of thoughts and wants)*

LORA: Well, I agree. I get nervous, too, about balancing the checkbook. *(expression of feelings)*

DON: Which reminds me, did you pick up the new checks from the bank today? We need to make sure they were printed correctly with our new address. *(straying off topic)*

LORA: That's another issue. Could we talk about some ideas first for solving the checkbook anxiety issue we seem to have? *(respectfully bringing Don back on topic)*

DON: You're right. That's more important. What do you think we should do? *(asking partner for her opinion)*

LORA: I think both of us keeping our own checkbooks is important. I don't want to have to ask you for checks. I've suggested before that we list all the checks each of us have written during the week and get together Sunday evening and put all the information together and balance the checkbook. But you have not agreed to do that, and so it's gone nowhere *(said respectfully)*. I'm not sure you like the idea. *(avoiding forcing your solution on your partner)*

DON: You sound disappointed that I haven't gotten back to you about your idea. *(empathic response)*

LORA: Yeah, I thought it was a good idea. Why don't we try it for a month and see if it helps? *(making a positive suggestion)*

DON: I'm willing to try it if you're first willing to read the brochure I brought home about budgeting your money, too. *(positive suggestion; willingness to compromise)*

LORA: OK. I know that budgeting is more important to you than it is to me, but I'm willing to learn. *(empathic response; willingness to compromise)*

For this couple, compromising worked well. When you compromise, each person yields or gives in a bit until together you find a middle ground or devise an alternative solution. Most conflicts in marriage can be negotiated this way.

Other Conflict Styles: The Good and the Bad

There are other styles of conflict resolution that couples use as well. I like Rusbult and Zembrodt's typology of conflict resolution, which concisely and scientifically describes these styles (see Figure 4.1).

Rusbult and Zembrodt use the terms *exit, voice, neglect,* and *loyalty.*

Exit refers to separating from one's spouse, leaving, moving out, or breaking up.

Voice refers to openly discussing problems, compromising, or changing oneself or requesting change from one's partner.

Loyalty refers to waiting and hoping that things will improve, praying for improvement, or supporting one's partner as he or she changes slowly.

Neglect refers to ignoring a problem, refusing to discuss it, being critical or insulting, or just letting things fall apart.

In the model, one dimension of conflict resolution is *activity-passivity,* which refers to the *impact* of the response of a partner on the problem being discussed, *not* to the nature of the behavior itself. For example, storming out of the room (exit) is

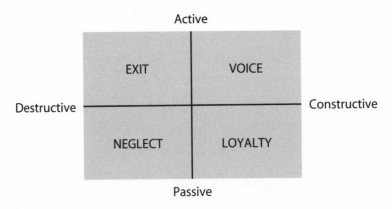

Figure 4.1. Styles of Conflict Resolution.[8]

an active behavior, but it is passively neglectful in regard to resolving the conflict because it is a refusal to discuss the problem. *Constructiveness-destructiveness* refers to the impact of your response on your marriage, not on you. For example, suddenly leaving the house while in conflict may be a constructive way for a spouse to handle anger at the moment, but such an exit is clearly destructive to the relationship. Thus exit and voice are active responses, whereas loyalty and neglect are passive with respect to the conflict itself.

As you might guess, marital satisfaction is related to using more constructive responses to conflict than destructive ones. The advantages of voice responses are self-evident. The loyalty response is constructive but more passive. This response approach is similar to accepting your partner or at least choosing your fights carefully. It may involve supporting your partner rather than trying to promote change, as well as refraining from criticism, giving the benefit of the doubt, and cultivating forgiveness—all responses that research shows improve marital satisfaction.

"Choosing your fights carefully" refers to making a conscious and deliberate choice of what issues in a relationship are worthy of a lengthy discussion and which ones are not worth the time, effort, and emotional cost to discuss. Examples of the former might be where you vacation, how to discipline the children, and what housework to share. Examples of the latter might be where to eat tonight, how messy the car is after your partner uses it, and your annoyance when you find clothes scattered all over the floor.

If you currently use one of the other two types of conflict responses—neglect or exit—chances are high that your marriage is dissatisfying and may not survive. In fact, these destructive ways of responding to conflict are more powerful determinants of your couple functioning than the constructive responses are. This may be because most of us expect our spouses to behave well, and so we take constructive responses for granted, whereas destructive responses produce far more negative emotions than constructive responses produce positive emotions.[9] Thus it is especially important to eliminate destructive response styles from your relationship.

Other Negative Communication Styles

Marital researcher John Gottman conducted some fascinating research in which he videotaped couples in conflict over a period of several years to discover what kinds of communication styles predict divorce.[10] He found that four patterns predict divorce: criticism, contempt, defensiveness, and stonewalling.

Criticism

When asking for change or commenting on your partner's negative behavior, you attack his personality or blame him for the problem. Your comments are generic rather than specific to the matter at hand and involve the frequent use of the term *you*—for example:

"You were late *again!* I can't trust you to do anything right, can I?"

"If you weren't so lazy, the dishes would have been done like I asked."

"What do I have to do, write down the directions or something? Even a child would have known how to find the Johnsons and deliver those clothes!"

Over time, criticism will destroy your marriage. Instead, you have to learn how to *complain*. Complaining does not involve a personal attack or blaming your partner. It is more specific. The term *I* is used—for example:

"I get frustrated when you're late. I would appreciate it if you would pay more attention to what time it is."

"It's frustrating to see those dishes when I get home. I thought you agreed to do them."

"Please tell me next time if you don't know the directions to the Johnsons."

Contempt

An even more vile insult to your partner is contempt. Here there is an intent to insult and psychologically abuse your partner. It's as if you cannot recall a single positive act or quality in your partner—for example:

"My mother warned me you would turn out to be a loser, but you don't even measure up to that standard!"

"Oh, yeah, you're God's gift to mankind, all right!"

"Why talk? You have *no* clue how I'm feeling. You wouldn't know a feeling if it walked up to you and shook your hand!"

Defensiveness

Defensiveness usually follows criticism and contempt as you try to defend yourself from your partner's barbs and insults. You may make excuses for your behaviors:

"I was late because the car was out of gas, as usual, because you've been driving it." Or you may cross-complain: "Well, I may be late *sometimes*, but you are *never* on time!"

Defensive statements rarely lead to understanding and resolving a problem in marriage. But defensiveness is a normal reaction when we feel criticized. It is much easier to be nondefensive if we hear a complaint expressed by our spouse rather than criticism or contempt.

Stonewalling

Individuals turn off their listening skills and remove themselves psychologically from a negative conversation when they feel emotionally or physically exhausted or overwhelmed by their spouse's attacks. They stop responding even defensively. Instead, they turn into a stone wall and keep silent even in the midst of criticism and contempt being heaped on them by their partner. This is a significant problem if it becomes habitual in your marriage. It is a major predictor of divorce.

In summary, if you discover one of these four negative communication styles in your marriage, make a commitment to stop the pattern *now*. This may require professional therapy if these patterns are chronic and serious.

⅋ Flooding and Soothing: A Negative Trait and a Positive Trait

You also need to be aware of two other conflict management processes in your marriage identified in Gottman's research. One, known as flooding, is negative, and the other, known as soothing, is positive.[11] Flooding refers to feeling overwhelmed with negative emotions and physically drained during an intense conflict with your partner. When you feel flooded, you need to take a break or a timeout to gather yourself, calm down, and be more rational. If your partner looks flooded, you can help by soothing her. An example of a soothing statement is "I see you're really upset now, and I don't want it to get any worse. Should we talk about this further later?" or "Why don't you take a few deep breaths and relax before going on any further with the point you were making." Gottman's research showed that happily married couples regularly recognize flooding and do something to stop it immediately: they soothe each other. Learn to recognize when you're feeling flooded, and learn to soothe your partner—both are skills you can learn.

Intimacy: The Reason We Got Married

If you ask most married people today why they got married, most will tell you, "To have a permanent, close, and intimate relationship." What does intimacy mean? It means several things, but primarily affection and sex.

Affection is expressed through kissing, hugging, caresses, holding hands, pats on the back, and other tender behavior. In addition, expressions like "I love you" or "You're the greatest" express affection. Gifts, notes, cards, flowers, candy, a fun lunch together, long talks on the porch about how much she means to you—all are examples of affection too. Affection keeps love alive. It is proof that you love her. It is a prerequisite for sex, especially for women.

People frequently ask marriage counselors, "How important is sex in marriage?" These are usually people whose sex lives are not very good. The best answer to this question is, it depends on the individual couple. For some couples sex is number one or number two in importance in determining their marital satisfaction. For others, sex is fourth or fifth or even lower in importance. If your sex life is good, you probably have few discussions about it. If it's bad, you likely have many discussions about it. In other words, "If you have a good sexual relationship, it's about 10% of the value of the relationship overall. If you don't have a good sexual relationship, it's about 90%."[12]

The good news is that most sexual problems are easily curable. Even the most common problems—lack of sexual desire, disagreement over the frequency of sexual relations, or mismatched sex drives—can be solved with self-help reading or professional marital or sex therapy (or a combination of the two). More about these resources can be found in Chapter Seven. The most important thing to remember is most people do *not* have to settle for a dissatisfying sexual relationship.

Consensus

Consensus refers to how much you agree or disagree on important life values. The greater the consensus and unity, the greater the marital intimacy and marital satisfaction. You just feel more like a unit when consensus is high. However, don't expect high consensus on everything. No two human beings see eye to eye on everything. Where there is a lack of consensus, you have two choices. First, agree to disagree— accept the difference and make adjustments in how you do things so that neither person feels coerced into doing it the other partner's way. For example, if you disagree on religious matters, each person can attend separate worship services. Second, resolve the difference by mutual give-and-take. For example, if you disagree on how often to have sex, take turns each month deciding how often. Or one partner chooses how often (taking into consideration your partner's feelings and needs) while the other chooses how. Be aware that not all differences in marriage are resolvable—acceptance is part of marriage, too. Some things we have to learn to live with and not let them drag us down emotionally or cause resentment.

One example of a difference that is not likely to change involves personality differences. If I'm outgoing and sociable and eager to party but my wife is more reserved and prefers a quiet evening at home by the fireplace to a night on the town, nothing I do will change this personality difference. The best strategy for a strong personality difference is to accept that we're different and learn to compromise on our weekend activities. For example, on one night we can go out with friends and go dancing, and the next night we can stay at home and catch up on our reading by the fireplace. Both of us are relatively happy, and she's glad I didn't drag her to a basketball game and pizza afterward the second night.

8 Cohesion

Cohesion refers to emotional and physical closeness, support in times of stress, and enjoying being together. It's part of the number one reason people get married, intimacy. However, spouses frequently vary on how much cohesion they want or are comfortable with. Here again, if there are differences in needs for closeness, compromises may have to be reached. These compromises include how often you go out together as a couple, with others, or individually. A good marriage does not require that you do everything together—you still both have friends and family you like to spend time with alone. *Balance* is the key. This means balancing togetherness and separateness so that both of you are happy. It's a key developmental task of early marriage. It's also a task of later marriage when the children no longer live at home.

There is no one right or wrong way to balance cohesion, but every couple must resolve it several times during the life of a marriage. If you have good communication and conflict resolution skills, you will be able to come to a mutual agreement on this issue. Good listening skills will also help you be more emotionally supportive of your partner and increase feelings of closeness in times of high stress or emotional upset.

⚘ Dealing with Power Problems

The sign of a satisfying marriage is not a *lack* of problems but rather the competent *handling* of problems. Of all the problems you checked on the Problem Areas Checklist on Worksheet 4.2, problems with who is in charge—power problems (item 72)—are perhaps the most important to resolve early in your marriage. Sharing power is most often defined as each spouse's having an equal say in making important decisions. These decisions include such matters as where to live, which job to take, how to manage money, how often to have sex, when to have children, which car to buy, where to go on vacation, and how to help children with college.

Does your partner share these decisions with you in a fair manner? What decisions do you defer to him to make without resentment or guilt on your part? The key emotion to look for that signals that your partner is not sharing power with you in your marriage is resentment. Or if you are the one taking more than your fair share of the power, you will likely frequently feel guilty about doing so.

Remember that unresolved power problems end up in bed with you. This was well illustrated by a comment a wife made to her husband in a therapy session with me. She said, "I don't feel close to you or even attracted to you when you boss me. If you really loved me, you would treat me like an equal. Only when I feel respected as an equal in your eyes will I feel affectionate and want to have sex with you." As you can see from her statement, sharing power is one of the foundations of intimacy.

If you look again at the Problem Areas Checklist, you will notice that not all problems are created equal. For example, household management problems are not as serious or marriage-threatening as power problems. Of all the other problems listed, four are most threatening to your marital satisfaction:

- Alcohol or substance abuse
- Other addictions (sex, gambling, eating, work, spending)
- Violence
- Infidelity

If you have a problem with one or more of these issues, professional therapy is *highly recommended.* The self-help resources in Chapter Seven of this book will probably not be enough to help you resolve these four serious problems. In Chapter Seven, I recommend how to find a qualified therapist for the treatment of these problems.

Be aware, too, that the presence of these problems does not necessarily mean that you should give up on your marriage and divorce. Many couples with these serious problems are able to overcome them and not just stay married but actually improve their marriage significantly.

🕈 Scoring and Interpretation Guidelines

You have reached the most important part of this chapter—evaluating and understanding your couple traits test results.

As in the previous chapter, for many of the short tests, the range of scores possible, the norm score, and significantly high or low scores are listed for you to consider. First, review your score sheets from Worksheet 4.1. Then respond to the questions on Worksheet 4.3. Finally, fill out Worksheet 4.4 so you have all your scores in front of you.

Communication and Conflict Resolution

There were three parts to your assessment of your current couple communication and conflict resolution skills:

1. Couple communication behavioral assessment exercise (already discussed)

2. Speaking and listening skills (short tests)

3. Conflict resolution styles (short tests)

You have completed your analysis of your behavioral assessment. For the next two sections, work from Worksheet 4.4. Based on your analysis of your scores, what are your communication skills strengths (scores that are at the norm or higher)? Areas for improvement (scores that are low)? What about your partner's strengths and areas for improvement?

_____

_____

_____

_____

_____

Each of you should answer the following questions, based on your answers on Worksheet 4.1. Then discuss your answers together as a couple.

1. Overall, how did this exercise go? What did you like about it? Dislike? What was the number one insight you gained?

_____

_____

_____

_____

2. Review items 1–9. What positive verbal behaviors did you do *most* frequently? What negative verbal behaviors did you do *most* frequently? What about your partner?

_____

_____

_____

_____

3. What was your ratio of positive skills to negative skills? Why?

_____

_____

_____

_____

4. How are the positive behaviors assets in your marriage? How are the negative behaviors liabilities?

_____

_____

_____

_____

Worksheet 4.3. Assessment of the Couple Communication Assessment Exercise.

5. What communication skills do you need to learn that will increase the effectiveness of your conflict resolution? What is the first step? Where can you get help?

_____

_____

_____

_____

6. Based on items 10–13, what were your most frequent positive and negative nonverbal behaviors? Which behaviors do you need to improve?

_____

_____

_____

_____

7. Look at your responses to items 14–16, and discuss your results. What improvements should be made in these three areas?

_____

_____

_____

_____

8. Based on your overall performance on the tape, how do you rate your couple conflict resolution skills? Do you have most of the skills necessary to effectively resolve conflicts? What skills do you need to learn or improve on? List them.

_____

_____

_____

_____

Worksheet 4.3. Assessment of the Couple Communication
Assessment Exercise, *Continued.*

Communication and Conflict Resolution

Items 1–12 on Worksheet 4.2 deal with speaking and listening skills. Write in your sum scores for each short test.

Trait	Range of Scores	Norm Score	Low Score	Your Score
Empathic communication (items 1–3)	3–15	11	9	_____
Clear sending (items 4–6)	3–15	11	9	_____
Partner's empathic communication (items 7–9)	3–15	11	9	_____
Partner's clear sending (items 10–12)	3–15	11	9	_____

Items 13–24 deal with conflict resolution response styles. Write in your sum scores for each short test.

Trait	Range of Scores	Norm Score	High Score[a]	Your Score
Exit response (items 13–15)	3–15	4	7	_____
Voice response (items 16–18)	3–15	10	13	_____
Loyalty response (items 19–21)	3–15	9	12	_____
Neglect response (items 22–24)	3–15	6	9	_____

Negative and Positive Communication Styles

Items 25–35 deal with negative communications styles, items 36–38 deal with flooding, and items 39–41 deal with a positive response to flooding, called soothing. Write in your sum scores for each short test.

Trait	Range of Scores	Norm Score	High Score	Your Score
Criticism (items 25–27)	3–15	6	8	_____
Contempt or defensiveness (items 28–31)	4–20	8	10	_____

Worksheet 4.4 Couple Traits Summary (Items 1–76).

[a]High scores are significant because they mean you use this style more frequently.

Trait	Range of Scores	Norm Score	Low Score	Your Score
Stonewalling (items 32–35)	4–20	8	10	_____
Flooding (items 36–38)	3–15	7	9	_____
Soothing (items 39–41)	3–15	7	9	_____

Intimacy

In the spaces provided, write your sum scores for the specified short tests you completed on Worksheet 4.2. These scores are your assessments of your marital intimacy, consensus, and cohesion.

Trait	Range of Scores	Norm Score	Low Score	Your Score
Intimacy: affection (items 42–44)	3–15	9	7	_____
Intimacy: sex (items 45–47)	3–15	9	7	_____
Consensus (items 48–53)	0–30	24	20	_____
Cohesion: closeness (items 54–56)	3–15	9	7	_____
Cohesion: togetherness (items 57–59)	3–15	9	7	_____
Overall marital satisfaction (items 60–62)	3–21	17	16	_____

Trait	Range of Scores	Norm Score	High Score	Your Score
Conventionality (items 63–65)	3–15	9	11	_____

Problem Areas Checklist

Rather than summing your scores on these items (66–76), list each problem you scored 3, 4, or 5.

_____	_____
_____	_____
_____	_____
_____	_____
_____	_____
_____	_____

Worksheet 4.4 Couple Traits Summary (Items 1–76), *Continued*

What skills do you want to enhance? How will you do that? (See the resources in Chapter Seven.)

_____

_____

_____

_____

_____

What is your most frequently used conflict resolution response style? Least frequently used style? How are these styles assets or liabilities in your marriage?

_____

_____

_____

_____

What changes do you need to make in your conflict resolution styles? What is the first step? Where can you get help learning new styles? (See Chapter Seven for resources.)

_____

_____

_____

_____

_____

Negative and Positive Communication Styles

Based on your analysis of your negative and positive communication styles, what negative styles do you use most frequently (scores in the high range)? Least frequently (scores below the norm)? How often do you use the positive style called soothing with your partner? What combination of negative and positive styles do you need to change in your marriage?

_____

_____

_____

_____

_____

Intimacy: Affection

Now let's look at your scores for the two intimacy tests, affection and sex, on Worksheet 4.4. For affection, what is your strength (scores at the norm or higher)? Area of concern (scores below the norm)? What about your sexual relationship? Describe below how you will improve affection and sex in your marriage. (See Chapter Seven for resources.)

_____

_____

_____

_____

_____

Consensus

Look at your total consensus score on Worksheet 4.4. How much consensus do you and your partner have on important issues in marriage (scores at the norm or higher)? Now look at each consensus item on Worksheet 4.2 (items 48–53), and tell how much consensus you think you have in each area. Topics rated 0–2 are low-consensus topics. How do you deal with these areas of disagreement? How can you improve the ways in which you deal with them? In what ways do the areas of agreement serve as strengths in your marriage?

_____

_____

_____

_____

_____

Cohesion

Look at your cohesion scores (closeness and togetherness) on Worksheet 4.4. How cohesive is your marriage (scores at or above the norm)? In what ways is it a strength or an area of concern? What can you do to build more cohesion in your marriage?

_____

_____

_____

_____

_____

Overall Marital Satisfaction

What is your overall level of marital satisfaction (see Worksheet 4.4)? How does your score compare to the norm score? Whose score is the higher, yours or your partner's? Scores of 16 or lower are a red flag and signal that you should consult with a marital therapist as soon as possible.

The timing of going to marriage therapy is analogous to going to your car mechanic as soon as you hear a strange noise in your engine. The sooner you take the car in and have the problem diagnosed and fixed, the better your chances of avoiding a bigger repair or an engine overhaul later. The same applies to your marriage. The sooner you go to therapy, the better your chances for saving your marriage with a tune-up rather than an expensive overhaul.

The problem for most couples going to marital therapy is that by the time they appear in the therapist's office, the problems have become chronic and difficult to treat. In fact, the average couple in therapy has had marriage problems for more than two years before seeking treatment. If you wait this long to get help, your mechanic may not be able to save your car!

Resources for finding a competent marital therapist are provided in Chapter Seven. Beware that *most* mental health professionals have *no* additional training or expertise in marital therapy, so you will need to be very cautious about whom you go to for therapy.

So what needs to be done concerning your overall marital satisfaction? Is the problem in a specific area like sex or consensus or communication skills? And what are your strengths?

_____

_____

_____

_____

_____

If you scored at or above the norm (17) on marital satisfaction, congratulations! However, even for you there may be a more specific area of marriage that needs enriching. It is not uncommon for happily married couples to have a specific area or two of their relationship that needs a tune-up even though, overall, they are happy. In what specific area do you need a tune-up?

_____

_____

_____

_____

_____

It is also possible that one of you scored significantly lower on overall marital satisfaction than the other. Since only one of you is relatively unsatisfied, does this mean that there is no need for marriage enrichment? Absolutely not! If *one* partner in a marriage is dissatisfied, it should be an issue for *both of you*. This is because marriage is a system, and if my partner is dissatisfied with one or more aspects of our marriage, even though I do not share her dissatisfaction in that area, her dissatisfaction will eventually cause me distress, too. A loving and committed spouse acknowledges his partner's complaints and takes a course of action (with her input) to improve the situation as best as he can. Perhaps an example of how this is done will help.

In a first marital therapy session, Micky (forty) and Joan (thirty-five) shared divergent versions of their marriage. Joan's overall marital satisfaction score (10) was significantly lower than Micky's score (18). The biggest problems were in the areas of cohesion and intimacy. Joan reported that their marriage was nearly affectionless. They also had not had sex in over a year. They had not been out on a date alone in three years. They reported spending one week away from the children nearly eight years before.

Micky said that overall, the marriage was fine for him. He came from an emotionally cold and distant family of origin and did not need much affection or sex, nor did he easily recognize or give Joan affection or sex. On other dimensions of marital satisfaction both partners scored relatively high (high consensus, good communication, and few problem areas).

At first Micky stated that the problems the couple described to me were not really *marriage* problems but rather *Joan's* problems. This hurt her deeply. She could not understand how he could stand by and see her so unfulfilled and sad and not try to change. Although Micky had a high cognitive IQ, his affection IQ and sex IQ were clearly below normal. Micky rationalized that since he had a low need for and understanding of affection and sex, Joan should just accept it and get off his back. This is when I had to teach Micky a valuable lesson about loving his wife: sometimes we need to change our behavior toward our partner *simply because she sincerely asks for a change.* Micky needed to drop his rationalizations and excuses and be more affectionate and sexual with Joan. Together we discussed how to do this, and his behavior improved. For him it was mainly a matter of learning to recognize his wife's affection needs better and then regularly fulfilling them, regardless of whether affection and sex were important to him. He and Joan also starting going out on a date alone every week and taking Sunday walks together without the children. The feelings of affection gained in these activities resulted in more frequent sex, too. A few lessons can be learned here:

1. If I truly love my partner and am committed to her for life, I sincerely listen to and acknowledge her complaints, even if I do not share the same thoughts, feelings, or needs.

2. Then I brainstorm with her how I can better meet her needs.

3. I choose a course of action to improve my behavior that is reasonable, based on my abilities, skills, and time, and execute it to the best of my ability.

4. I ask for feedback from her on how I'm improving.

As a result of this process, I have a happier spouse and I feel better about myself, too. *Both of us* increase our marital satisfaction this way. So if your spouse is asking for a change, what are you willing to do now?

_____

_____

_____

_____

_____

If you are requesting change from your partner, how are you doing it? Taking a loving and patient attitude? Using good communication skills? Using a voice conflict resolution style?

_____

_____

_____

_____

_____

Marital Conventionality

How conventional are you when it comes to evaluating your marital satisfaction? Conventionality refers to answering questions about your marriage in a socially desirable way—in other words, in a way that makes you and your marriage look better than it really is. It is a human tendency to overrate ourselves and our relationships or paint an overly rosy picture of our marriage.

Look at your conventionality score (see Worksheet 4.4, items 63–65). How high is it? The higher the score, the more you answered the questions about your marriage in a conventional or unrealistically positive manner. If your score was over 8, you were looking at your marriage through really thick rose-colored glasses.

Individuals do this for a reason—most of us do not want to admit that our marriage is not perfect or at least OK. But the problem here is that you cannot improve your marriage if you cannot first look at it realistically.

Who scored higher on conventionalization, you or your partner? Why? What can you do to be more objective about your problems?

_____

_____

_____

_____

_____

_____

Problem Areas

Look at Worksheet 4.2, and see which items are problems for you today. Each of you should list here the three most important problems (the three you scored the highest) that need to be discussed and resolved. How does your list match your partner's list? Select the one problem you both agree to work on *now*. Discuss how you will begin resolving this problem. Write your plan here. If it seems overwhelming to do this, plan to discuss it with a professional therapist present to help you.

_____

_____

_____

_____

_____

_____

❧ More Serious Marital Problems

Items 77–79 assess violence in marriage. If you rated any of these items 2 or 3, you need to discuss when and where to get professional help to overcome them. This is because these are the most serious and dangerous of all marriage problems to solve. Refer to Chapter Seven for recommendations on where to find a therapist. Note that not all marital therapists *specialize* in treating violence. You will need to interview potential therapists from a list and ask for specific treatment for violence in marriage.

Items 80–82 should be treated the same way. They measure problems with alcohol or drugs. Any item scored 2 or 3 means you or your partner may have a substance abuse problem that needs treatment. See Chapter Seven for recommendations on locating a chemical dependency counselor. Note that not all mental health professionals have training in treating these problems. Again, careful interviewing by you, the client, will be necessary to get proper treatment. If you circled "yes" on item 83, see a marital therapist soon. An affair creates a crisis in a marriage serious enough that most couples require professional assistance to overcome the many problems it creates. Do *not* assume that infidelity should necessarily lead to divorce. Many couples have successfully repaired their marriage and stayed together.

❧ Your Big Picture

Finally, based on all of the couple assessments and written responses in this chapter, list your *couple* traits that are assets and liabilities:

Assets   *Liabilities*

_____   _____

_____   _____

_____   _____

_____   _____

_____   _____

_____   _____

_____   _____

_____   _____

_____   _____

_____   _____

What does this list mean to you? Where do you need a tune-up the most? What can you do next? Who can help you? When will you start?

_____

_____

_____

_____

_____

Congratulations! You have now finished assessing the second factor in the Marriage Triangle—your couple traits. In the next chapter you will learn about and assess contextual traits that predict marital satisfaction. Continue to be open-minded and objective in answering these questions and discussing the results with your partner.

Factor 3

Your Personal and Relationship Contexts

Although we have four children, we consciously make time to be alone every week for private couple time. Without it, we would lose track of each other.

—Nancy, thirty-seven-year-old pharmacist

After three years of fighting over her parents' interfering with our marriage, we finally sat down and called a truce. Their interference was destroying our relationship. It was time we drew a line with them.

—Gene, twenty-nine-year-old construction worker

My parents had a conflicted and unhappy marriage. So when I got married, I had only their faulty blueprint to follow. It's not working.

—Janice, thirty-year-old investment banker

These individuals' statements emphasize the strong effects that personal and relationship contexts can have on one's marriage. Context refers to the environment in which your marriage functions (see Figure 2.2). Personal context refers to family-of-origin influences we each bring into marriage with us that form a backdrop for how we interact in marriage—a happy parental marriage or a bitter parental divorce, functional family relationships or dysfunctional family dynamics such as abuse, neglect, or poor communication. They also include family process leftovers—bad memories or emotional remnants of things that happened to us in our family—that still bother us and affect the way we regard others and interact with them. An example of such a leftover is the long-term effects of childhood neglect or abuse. Individuals who have experienced abuse in childhood frequently have low self-esteem as adults, mistrust others, and bond insecurely with their spouses. Finally, autonomy, or healthy psychological independence from your family of origin, is an important predictor of your subsequent marital satisfaction.

Your relationship contexts include outside stressors that affect your marriage, such as financial, work, and parenting stress. It also includes in-laws and their positive and negative influences on your marriage. Together, personal and relationship contexts can put enormous stress on an otherwise healthy marriage. Likewise, they can enrich your marriage if they are good. Your marriage probably has a mixture of positive and negative contexts.

The purpose of this chapter is to explain how the following contexts affect marital satisfaction:

Personal Contexts

1. Family of origin influences

2. Family process leftovers

3. Parental marriage as a model

4. Parental divorce

5. Autonomy from family of origin

Relationship Contexts

1. Outside stressors

2. Work stress

3. Outside interests competition

4. Parenting stress

5. Parental and friends' approval and support

6. In-law influences

Before delving into the positive and negative influences contexts can exert on your marriage, let's do an assessment of your personal and relationship contexts by completing the short tests on Worksheet 5.1. At the end of the chapter I will show you how to use your scores and responses on Worksheet 5.1 to determine your strengths and areas for improvement from your contexts.

	Strongly Disagree	Disagree	Undecided	Agree	Strongly Agree

Overall Evaluation of Family of Origin

1. From what I experienced in my family of origin, I think family relationships are safe, secure, rewarding, worth being in, and a source of comfort.   1   2   3   4   5

2. From what I experienced in my family, I think family relationships are confusing, unfair, anxiety-provoking, inconsistent, and unpredictable.   1   2   3   4   5

3. We had a loving atmosphere in our family.   1   2   3   4   5

4. All things considered, my childhood years were happy.   1   2   3   4   5

First, reverse the score for item 2. For example, if you circled 1, score it as 5; if you circled 2, score it as 4; 3 remains the same. Then sum your responses to items 1–4, and write your score here: _____

Parents' Marriage

5. My father was happy in his marriage.   1   2   3   4   5

6. My mother was happy in her marriage.   1   2   3   4   5

7. I would like my marriage to be like my parent's marriage.   1   2   3   4   5

Sum your responses to items 5–7, and write your score here: _____

Family Process Leftovers

8. There are matters from my family experience that I'm still having trouble dealing with and coming to terms with.   1   2   3   4   5

Worksheet 5.1. Assessing Contexts.[1]

	Strongly Disagree	Disagree	Undecided	Agree	Strongly Agree

9. There are matters from my family experience that negatively affect my ability to form close relationships. 1 2 3 4 5

10. I feel at peace about anything negative that happened to me in the family I grew up in. 1 2 3 4 5

Reverse-score items 8 and 9; then sum your responses to items 8–10, and write your score here: _____

My Autonomy

11. My parents currently encourage me to be independent and make my own decisions. 1 2 3 4 5

12. My parents currently try to run my life. 1 2 3 4 5

Reverse-score item 12; then sum your responses to items 11–12, and write your score here: _____

Parental Conflict Management Style

13. The following is a description of how some parents handle conflict in marriage: My parents argued often and hotly. There were a lot of insults back and forth, name-calling, put-downs, and sarcasm. They didn't really listen to what the other was saying, nor did they look at each other very much. One or the other of them could be quite detached and emotionally uninvolved, even though there may have been brief episodes of attack and defensiveness. There were clearly more negatives than positives in their relationship.

    How often did your parents use this style? *(Circle one letter.)*

    A. Never
    B. Rarely
    C. Sometimes
    D. Often
    E. Very often

Worksheet 5.1. Assessing Contexts, *Continued*

Abuse in the Family

14. Sometimes in families, conflicts can lead to physical acts that are violent. These acts may include slapping, pushing, kicking, hitting hard with a fist, hitting with objects, or other types of violence. Considering all of your experiences while growing up in your family, how would you rate the general level of violence in your home? *(Circle one letter.)*

   A. There was never violence in the home.
   B. There was rarely violence in the home.
   C. There was sometimes violence in the home.
   D. There was often violence in the home.
   E. There was very often violence in the home.

15. Sometimes in families, sexual activities occur that are inappropriate. These acts may include a parent or sibling fondling a child, a parent or sibling engaging in sexual intercourse with a child, or some other type of inappropriate sexual activity. Considering all of your experiences while growing up in your family, how often did one or more of these inappropriate sexual activities happen to you? *(Circle one letter.)*

   A. Never
   B. Rarely
   C. Sometimes
   D. Often
   E. Very often

16. How often was someone outside your family (not your current partner) sexually abusive toward you? *(Circle one letter.)*

   A. Never
   B. Rarely
   C. Sometimes
   D. Often
   E. Very often

Family Structure

17. Circle the letter indicating the type of family situation in which you spent the most time while growing up (to age eighteen).

   A. One parent because of divorce
   B. One parent because of death
   C. Both biological parents
   D. A parent and a stepparent
   E. A foster family
   F. An adoptive family
   G. A relative (for example, grandparent)

Worksheet 5.1. Assessing Contexts. *Continued*

Parents' and Friends' Approval

How much do the following individuals currently approve of your marriage

	Not at All	Somewhat	Mostly	Entirely
18. Your father	1	2	3	4
19. Your mother	1	2	3	4
20. Your friends	1	2	3	4
21. Your partner's father	1	2	3	4
22. Your partner's mother	1	2	3	4
23. Your partner's friends	1	2	3	4

In-Law Stress

	Very Unhappy	Unhappy	Undecided	Happy	Very Happy
24. How happy are you with your mother-in-law?	1	2	3	4	5

	Very Little	Little	Some	Much	Very Much
25. How much conflict, tension, or disagreement do you feel there is between you and your mother-in-law?	1	2	3	4	5

	Never	Seldom	Sometimes	Often	Very Often
26. How often do you feel your mother-in-law makes too many demands on you?	1	2	3	4	5

Reverse-score item 24; then sum your responses to items 24–26, and write your score here: _____

Worksheet 5.1. Assessing Contexts. *Continued*

	Very Unhappy	Unhappy	Undecided	Happy	Very Happy
27. How happy are you with your father-in-law?	1	2	3	4	5

	Very Little	Little	Some	Much	Very Much
28. How much conflict, tension, or disagreement do you feel there is between you and your father-in-law?	1	2	3	4	5

	Never	Seldom	Sometimes	Often	Very Often
29. How often do you feel your father-in-law makes too many demands on you?	1	2	3	4	5

Reverse-score item 27; then score your responses to items 27–29, and write your score here: _____

Perceived Stress

	Never	Seldom	Sometimes	Often	Very Often
30. In the past month, how often have you felt that you were unable to control the important things in your life?	1	2	3	4	5
31. In the past month, how often have you felt conflict about your ability to handle your personal problems?	1	2	3	4	5
32. In the past month, how often have you felt that things were going your way?	1	2	3	4	5

Reverse-score item 32; then sum your responses to items 30–32, and write your score here: _____

Worksheet 5.1. Assessing Contexts. *Continued*

Stress Sources

33. List the three major sources of your current stress (financial problems, illness, death of a loved one, job loss, children's problems, and so on):

_____

_____

_____

_____

Parenting Stress

Circle Your Responses:

	Strongly Disagree	Disagree	Undecided	Agree	Strongly Agree
34. We seldom go out as a couple because it's more important to spend time with our children.	1	2	3	4	5
35. We take our children almost everywhere with us, so we have little "couple time" alone.	1	2	3	4	5
36. By the time we get the children settled at night, there is no time left for just the two of us.	1	2	3	4	5

Sum your responses to items 34–36, and write your score here: _____

Work Stress

Mark each item as it applies to you, your spouse, or both of you.

	Strongly Disagree	Disagree	Undecided	Agree	Strongly Agree
37. We spend so much time at work that we have little time left to spend together as a couple.	1	2	3	4	5
38. Work stresses me out to the point that I have little energy left for our relationship.	1	2	3	4	5

Worksheet 5.1. Assessing Contexts. *Continued*

	Strongly Disagree	Disagree	Undecided	Agree	Strongly Agree
			Circle Your Responses:		

39. I get the feeling that work is more important for us than our marriage.   1   2   3   4   5

Sum your responses to items 37–39, and write your score here: _____

Outside Interests Stress

Mark each item as it applies to you, your spouse, or both of you.

40. Hobbies, sports, or other recreation activities routinely interfere with time we could spend together as a couple.   1   2   3   4   5

41. Getting too involved in individual outside activities is a problem in our marriage.   1   2   3   4   5

42. Time together as a couple is less important than our individual hobbies, recreation, or interests.   1   2   3   4   5

Sum your responses to items 40–42, and write your score here: _____

Worksheet 5.1. Assessing Contexts. *Continued*

❧ Personal Context: Family-of-Origin Influences

The Role of Your Parent's Marriage

Our longitudinal research with the RELATE instrument has shown a consistent positive relationship between healthy family-of-origin functioning and an individual's marital satisfaction. This relationship has held true even in older couples. Certain types of family relationship experiences either hinder or enhance your marital satisfaction. The family factors most likely to *enhance* your marriage include whether your parents' marriage was a happy one. Their marriage is a blueprint or model for you to follow in your own marriage. Their communication skills, conflict resolution style, ways of expressing affection, and other interactions are likely to have been passed down to you. They are your role models for how husbands and wives behave in marriage. That does not mean you automatically follow their pattern, but their influence is great.

If you or your spouse witnessed chronic hostile marital conflict while growing up, you are less likely than others to have developed good communication skills and conflict resolution skills (assessed in Chapter Four). Your response as a child to chronic hostile conflict was likely anxiety and depression. The lessons in your head taken from witnessing such negative parental conflict might include these:

- Married people fight.
- Marriage is dangerous.
- Marriage is difficult, leading to hurt and resentment.
- Disagreements are bad because they always result in fights and hurt feelings.

These messages may be imprinted in your mind and influence your behavior when you try to resolve conflict with your spouse.

Perhaps your parents did not fight but were nevertheless very dissatisfied with their marriage. Such chronic unhappiness may have taught you lessons about marriage like these:

- Marriage is unfulfilling—you just put up with each other.
- Marriage is painful.
- Married people are long-suffering.
- People get stuck in marriage.

Such lessons may be difficult to erase from your mind and can lessen your marital satisfaction if not eradicated or modified.

Hostile Parental Conflict Management

The conflict management style you learned from your parents will likely transfer into your own marriage. After all, your parents served as your role models for conflict resolution. One style that hinders effective conflict management in marriage is a hostile attack-and-defend style with a goal to hurt the other person. Another style that seldom works is called conflict-phobic, involving an intense fear of conflict or disagreement. Spouses who adopt this style simply refuse to deal with issues openly, often because they are afraid they cannot solve them or are uncomfortable with conflict. Frustration, anger, and resentment are often the results of lingering unresolved conflict.

Marital researcher John Gottman has found that happily married couples usually resolve conflict in one of four ways.[2] Three of them seem to work and to contribute to marital satisfaction. The first successful type is called *volatile*. Volatile couples engage in discussions in an enthusiastic manner. They do not try to understand or empathize with each other; rather, each spouse tries to persuade the other. For them, "winning is what it's all about." Their conflicts are volcanic but just a small part of an otherwise warm and loving marriage.

A second successful approach Gottman calls the *avoidant* style. Conflict avoiders minimize their differences rather than resolving them. They neither attempt to persuade nor to compromise; very little gets settled. They "agree to disagree." They make light of their differences. However, this pattern does *not* lead to marital dissatisfaction. Rather than resolve conflicts, these couples "appeal to their basic shared philosophy of marriage." They love each other, accentuate the positives, and accept their differences. This style is different from the phobic style mentioned earlier, where spouses do not even *try* to resolve differences. In that case, there is literally no discussion of problems because of a lack of communication skills, high anxiety, or chronic discouragement from never solving their conflicts.

The third successful style is called the *validating* style. This is the style that marriage counselors think is the ideal. We try to teach couples this style in counseling and marriage enrichment workshops. Validators listen to each other respectfully, and after both partners feel they have fully aired their opinions, they each attempt to gain the other's agreement. Attempts to convince each other are good-natured, with no arm-twisting. Many times these couples resolve conflicts with compromise.

The fourth approach to conflict resolution described by Gottman is characteristic of unhappily married couples and is referred to as *hostile*. Couples who use this style insult each other. Neither person listens. The arguments usually end in hurt feelings and resentment. This conflict pattern predicts divorce for most couples.

The Impact of Parental Divorce

Researchers are not sure how long the negative effects of divorce on children or teenagers last, but they certainly last at least into early marriage. Individuals whose parents divorced (especially if it was a highly conflicted marriage and divorce) are somewhat more likely to divorce than individuals whose parents had stable marriages.[3] There are many plausible reasons for this relationship; three have substantial research support.

First, compared to people from intact families, the offspring of families of divorce have a greater willingness to resort to divorce themselves as a solution to marital problems. Their parents' divorce served as a role model for divorce for them. Although divorce is almost always painful, they witnessed their parents' surviving the process intact.

Second, they also have a lower commitment to marriage, perhaps thinking, "If my parents' marriage failed, mine can too. Since marriage is fragile, I'd better not put all my eggs in one basket," or, "Like my dad, I'll give this marriage a good shot, but if it doesn't work out, I can easily get out at any time." Divorce, then, is more plausible to children of divorce than to children of intact marriages. This lowers their level of commitment to working out problems with their partner and may make them less optimistic about solving marital problems. Thus they may be more likely to resort to divorce.

Third, children of divorce may develop interpersonal behaviors that hinder marital satisfaction. These include problems with anger, jealousy, hurt feelings, mistrust, communication, or infidelity. These problems stem from both poor parental marital quality and parental divorce. Such problematic interpersonal behaviors may increase your risk of divorce.[4]

An example of how these factors combine to impede the resolution of marital problems can be seen in Paul and Jane's twelve-year marriage. Both Paul and Jane are thirty-seven years old. Paul's parents went through a bitter divorce when he was thirteen. When problems arose in year nine of his own marriage, he reported remembering his father's advice to him soon after his parents' divorce: "Don't trust women—ultimately, they will leave you and take all they can get their hands on." He also had vivid memories of his parents' hostile conflict and anger. He never witnessed a healthy resolution of differences between his parents. This legacy made him very anxious when he and Jane developed their own problems. He had difficulty committing to marriage counseling, and his mistrust of Jane and her intentions and commitment to the marriage surfaced frequently in the counseling sessions. Jane tried to convince him that she was not like his mother and that he should not adopt his father's negative attitude about wives. Paul also struggled to imagine how a couple might argue constructively and without hurting each other. Fortunately, he was open to learning a conflict resolution style much different from his parents', and he and Jane were eventually able to discuss their problems in a healthy way, with some professional assistance.

Overcoming the Negative Effects of Divorce

Lest this divorce discussion discourage you if you are a child of divorce, let me offer some reassuring comments. First, if you or your partner exhibits problematic behaviors or "emotional allergies" inherited from your parents' divorce but your partner has good communication skills, is trusting, and is highly committed to the relationship, your chances for marital satisfaction improve greatly.[5] Second, if you are already aware of these problems (for example, problems trusting your spouse), you can learn through professional therapy how to overcome them and how to act in more appropriate ways.

In addition, you should not interpret this discussion to mean that divorce is inevitable for the children of divorce or that persons from divorced families should not marry. These are the crucial questions you must ask yourself or your partner if you come from a divorced family: How did your parents' marital dissatisfaction and divorce affect you emotionally at the time it occurred? How do you feel about it now? How did your parents' marital dissatisfaction and divorce affect your development of communication and conflict resolution skills? What are your attitudes about commitment in marriage? About divorce? How did your parents' divorce affect these attitudes? What unresolved feelings or problems with trust, jealousy, anger, and other emotions you need to deal with are related to their divorce? Write your answers here:

_____

_____

_____

_____

It is interesting to note that in some cases parental divorce has a positive effect on children affected by it: it may motivate them to develop better communication skills or to commit more fully to their own marriage than their parents did.

Other Family-of-Origin Effects

Other family-of-origin experiences may have a positive influence on your marriage.[6] One is if your relationship with your parents was satisfying, affectionate, and emotionally close. This leads to positive self-esteem, confidence about relationships, trusting others, a desire to become intimate and emotionally close to others, and the ability to make long-term commitments in relationships.

Another is if as an adult, you feel a healthy sense of independence from your parents. For example, you do not feel as if they are trying to run your life or involve you in trying to solve their problems for them. In other words, are you emotionally connected to your parents but not *enmeshed* (too close to them) or *disengaged* (too distant from them) emotionally? Emotional independence in the family of origin frees you to develop an intimate relationship with your spouse. It is a healthy result of personality development but sometimes does not occur until after you are married.

A third positive influence is if your family communication is open and honest without being hurtful. This shows that you have learned how to express yourself appropriately, listen well, and resolve conflicts in a healthy way.

By contrast, two family factors are the most likely ones to inhibit your marital satisfaction:

- If your relationship with your parents was unsatisfying, emotionally cold, detached, neglectful, or abusive

- If your parents are emotionally enmeshed or overinvolved in your life, controlling or intimidating you, or overly emotionally dependent on you

Perhaps an example of these latter family dynamics will be useful here.

The Enmeshed Son

Early in my career, I saw a young couple whose major complaint after a year of marriage involved the husband's family-of-origin problems, which had started long before their wedding. The problem was that the husband's parents had an unsatisfying, conflictual marriage. The problem was chronic—it had lasted for more than twenty years, yet they were still married. When the arguments got too hot, my client's mother would call her son and ask him to come over for a meal or some other social gathering. While at the meal or gathering, both parents would pull my client aside and take turns complaining about the other, each parent trying to win him over to his or her side. His mother divulged that he had always "helped keep their marriage together" and that she "didn't know what she would do" without his help. This led him to feel depressed when his mother felt so bad. Their emotional lives were enmeshed.

Needless to say, these visits to his family of origin caused a great deal of anxiety for him and his wife. His wife accompanied him on these occasions, but he virtually ignored her while he was doing his amateur marriage counseling. He would return home after a visit angry and frustrated at his parents, and she would return hurt and resentful that her husband ignored her and let himself get caught up in a problem that his parents should solve on their own.

This couple came to me because of the tension and disruption the enmeshment with his family of origin caused them as a couple. The wife demanded that he cut off this unhealthy relationship with his family. But he felt too guilty and anxious about his parents' marriage and his role in resolving their problems to act appropriately by setting firmer boundaries.

The husband was a bit shocked when I suggested that he turn over his marriage-counseling role to a licensed professional, but ultimately a great sense of relief came to both of their faces when he finally agreed. Getting himself out of this dysfunctional, enmeshed family-of-origin situation gave him more emotional strength and time to develop his role as a husband in his young marriage.[7]

Child Abuse Effects

The most serious family-of-origin influences on your marriage are child neglect or abuse and parental alcohol or drug dependency. Neglect and abuse damage a person's self-esteem and may lead to chronic depression, anxiety, resentment, and anger toward parents or more serious mental health problems that can poison a marriage. Parental alcohol or drug dependency damages the parent's ability to provide a stable, predictable, and healthy parent-child relationship and a satisfying marriage. The results of the damage to the psychological and interpersonal functioning of the offspring of alcoholics is seen in the higher divorce rate for adult children of alcoholics compared to adult children of nonalcoholics. And many of these adult children become alcoholics themselves. Later in this chapter I discuss how to overcome the effects of these kinds of dysfunctional family patterns on you and your marital adjustment.

To clarify, here is another example of the effects of child abuse on one's later marital satisfaction.[8] A couple in their late twenties came to me for help with the problem of chronic conflict over when to have children, how many children to have, and how to raise them. This couple currently had one three-year-old son. Both the husband and the wife traced the conflict between them back to the wife's experiences in her family of origin. While the wife was growing up, her mother told her that she was ugly and fat and that no "normal boy" would ever want her. Her mother even listened to her telephone calls to boyfriends and teased her about them. Earlier in life, the woman had also physically abused her daughter.

In therapy, the wife explained to me, "I learned as a child that children are to be despised, never wanted. I never felt wanted. So why would *I* want another child? Why would *anyone* want to be a parent? I guess my husband will just have to raise our three-year-old. I can't!"

This is a tragic story because this young mother was failing to bond with her son. An absence of healthy mother-child bonding can lead to serious psychological problems for children. The father felt inadequate to provide enough emotional support for his son to make up the difference. He threatened to divorce his wife if she did not deal with her issues from the past and be a better mother to their son. As a result, she entered therapy, which eventually led to her reconciling with her mother and forgiving the woman for the past. Not all stories of the effects of childhood abuse in adulthood are this bad; yet some are even worse. The point is that abuse frequently traumatizes a person to the point that without professional therapy, the individual will have a higher-than-average chance of having marital difficulties.

It is a tribute to the resilience of the human spirit that some neglect and abuse victims suffer few psychological problems or later marital problems even without professional therapy. Social scientists are just beginning to understand the resiliency or hardiness some individuals exhibit.

Indirect Effects of Family of Origin on Marriage

I said earlier that family-of-origin issues might have a more indirect than direct effect on your later marital satisfaction. Figure 5.1 shows why this effect may be indirect. In research, we seldom find a strong direct relationship (straight arrow) between family-of-origin processes (box A) and the marital satisfaction of offspring (box C). Rather, we usually find a stronger relationship between family-of-origin processes (for example, family cohesion, abuse, alcoholism), on the one hand, and one's personality and self-esteem (individual traits) and couple communication skills (couple traits), on the other. These intermediate factors in turn affect one's marital satisfaction. This shows how the enduring strength and influence of family factors at the base of the Marriage Triangle may affect your later marital satisfaction. The dashed line between box A and box C represents this indirect but nonetheless important relationship between family-of-origin processes and marital satisfaction. The relationship is said to be indirect because the factors in box A affect box C through box B. What family-of-origin processes described in this chapter have affected your personality, self-esteem, and communication skills? How does this increase or decrease your marital satisfaction? Write your responses here:

_____

_____

_____

_____

_____

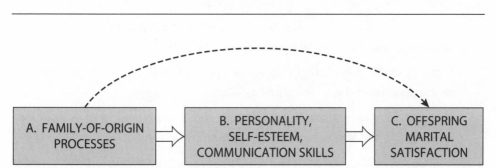

Figure 5.1. Impact of Family of Origin.

❧ Relationship Context: Stressors Affecting Marriage

The second category of contexts that influence your marriage for better or worse is referred to as the relationship context. This includes the effects of the following environmental influences on you and your marriage:

- Parents' and friends' approval of your marriage

- In-laws

- Stress from parenting, careers, and outside interests

Each of these can be liabilities or assets in your marriage. For example, good in-law relationships can strengthen your marriage, and bad in-law relationships weaken your marriage. Stress is a natural part of life, and we must all develop good stress management skills to keep our sanity and protect our marriage.

Let's look first at the importance of other's approval of your marriage and in-law issues.

Others' Approval of Your Marriage

Marriage doesn't take place in a vacuum: you don't just marry a person; you marry a whole family. Thus your parents' and your partner's parents' opinions and approval of your marriage are important to your marital satisfaction. Lack of parental support for your marriage can add much stress to your relationship and is related to marital dissatisfaction and divorce. This is especially true if the parents are very vocal about it!

Parental approval of your marriage helps you in a number of ways:

- It validates your marriage. It is reassuring when the most important people in your life validate your spouse and your relationship.

- It increases the chances that they will support you and your spouse when problems arise and you need their assistance.

- It makes them more likely to compliment your partner and your wise choice in a mate. In this way it builds both spouses' self-esteem.

Friend's approval is important for the same reasons.

What if your parents or friends disapprove of your marriage? What should you do? The key is *balance*—balancing your own feelings and opinions with those of your parents and friends. If their feelings and opinions differ greatly from your own, I suggest the following:[9]

- Keep an open mind—you don't have to accept or agree with their opinion to hear them.

- Take time to consider the feedback you are receiving from family and friends. Is there consensus among them?

- If you and your parents or friends still disagree about your marriage ideas, try getting the opinion of a more objective third party, for example, a clergy person or a therapist.

- If all parties, including the more objective ones, agree, seek professional therapy. Some individuals (such as victims of abusive spouses or spouses of alcoholics) cannot see the damage that a dysfunctional marriage relationship is causing them personally.

Realistic examples of the negative effects of parental disapproval on marriages have been portrayed in two popular movies, *Love Story* and *She's Having a Baby*. Both movies are about a couple falling in love, marrying, and adjusting in the first year of marriage.

In *Love Story* (the more serious example), there is a strong parental disapproval of the marriage from both sides of the family. The couple—Jenny and Oliver—marry anyway. The negative effects of this disapproval on the marriage are painful to watch. In one scene, the new wife is talking to her husband's father about his upcoming birthday party. Jenny holds out the phone and asks Oliver to talk directly to his father. Oliver refuses because of built-up resentment for his father's disapproving the marriage and putting down Jenny's blue-collar background. This causes Jenny and Oliver to have an explosive argument that results in Jenny's leaving the apartment in tears.

The negative effects of parental disapproval are more humorously illustrated in the dark comedy *She's Having a Baby*. The disapproval starts when Kristi brings Jake home to meet her family for the first time and continues unmercifully through their marriage and the birth of their first child. Each time the couple needs emotional or financial support from their parents, little is given because of their continuing opposition. This puts great stress on the marriage. It also damages both parties' self-esteem.

Depending on the mood you are in, select one of these movies to watch, and then discuss the effects of parental disapproval with your partner.

In-Laws and Marriage

Approval of your marriage from your parents is important, but there's more to the picture than that. You have to get along with your in-laws, too. People used to think that in-law problems cropped up only among newlyweds. Recent research shows that even after twenty-five years of marriage, relationships with in-laws can have a significant effect—positive or negative—on your marital satisfaction.[10]

In-laws are able to influence spouses in at least two notable ways. First, you are obligated to form a family bond with these "nonblood kin." This forced relationship is rarely a natural match of kindred spirits.[11] Second, in-laws can create hostility and stress between spouses who have emotional and psychological loyalties to their own families. In fact, some spouses never truly feel comfortable with their in-laws.

Alternatively, in-laws can be a source of love and support for you and your partner. Many husbands even develop a friendshiplike relationship with their fathers-in-law; similarly close bonds may develop between wives and their mothers-in-law. In some situations, your relationship with your same-sex in-law may even rival or exceed that of your relationship with your own parent.

Regardless, an important developmental task for marriage is developing healthy in-law relations and coming to an agreement with your spouse on which set of in-laws or parents they enjoy visiting and the frequency of such get-togethers. Another issue is boundaries. How firm is the privacy boundary around your marriage? How much do you want your parents and in-laws to know about your marriage? Every couple must come to an agreement on this issue, too.

An example of this issue occurred with Wendy (thirty-five) and John (thirty-eight). Wendy had an especially close relationship with her mother and did not wish to lessen it much after marriage. John accepted that, and they visited her mother every week. However, when Wendy started sharing details of their marriage problems with her mother, John became incensed. Talking about their marriage with her mother violated his privacy boundary, and it took him and Wendy several hours of discussion to come to a couple boundary agreement about how much Wendy would disclose about their marriage when her mother asked, "So how are the two of you doing, dear?"

The important points here are these:

- Remember that your first allegiance is to your spouse, not to your parents. Your spouse's needs must come first.

- Come to an agreement on your couple boundary with your parents and in-laws.

- Be positive and flexible about visiting your in-laws. Remember that conflicting loyalties are not uncommon for you or your partner. Partners cannot simply cut off their relationships with parents when they get married. Balancing the relationship with them is key, but the marriage comes first.

For some good ideas for solving in-law problems, see Bill Doherty's book *Take Back Your Marriage*.[12]

If in-laws become too intrusive in your marriage, you should set limits and then calmly enforce them.[13] If they violate the limits, you may have to stay away from them for a while to reinforce your stand. But be respectful and patient. If necessary, tell them plainly your minimum expectations for their treatment of your partner, and hold firm to those expectations.

Good relationships with in-laws are a bonus when marrying your partner. The four of you can have good times together, and they can be very supportive of your marriage in times of stress or difficulty. They may even make sacrifices to help you enrich your marriage. An example of this comes from my own marriage.

One September, Jeannie and I went to Rome on a ten-day romantic vacation. At the time, we had two school-aged children at home with busy extracurricular lives. Jeannie's parents, Jay and Ruby, came up from Arizona to stay at our house for the ten-day period and serve as substitute parents. As a result, Jeannie and I enjoyed our trip without any worries or concerns about our children's welfare, karate classes, church activities, school, the condition of the house, or anything else on the domestic front. Jay and Ruby even made the kids follow their regular household chore chart and gave them their allowances! As a result of my in-laws' unselfish service, we had the best trip of our lives. And the kids got better acquainted with their grandparents. Jay and Ruby have been an unexpected but wonderful bonus that came with my wife in my marriage.

Many in-laws are similarly generous—giving emotional, physical, and financial support to their sons-in-law and daughters-in-law. I even know a few who helped their children save their marriage by providing good counsel and encouragement during a marital crisis. My advice is do all you can to foster such support from your in-laws and parents.

Unmanaged Stress: An Enemy to Marriage

Another important and powerful negative influence on your marital satisfaction is unmanaged or poorly managed stress. Here I am talking about stress from outside sources: job-related stress, commuting, dealing with frustrating people, taking care of the house and children, everyday crises and hassles, expected and unexpected changes (such as relocation or illness), car trouble, and so on. The list is endless.

The interesting thing about this list of stressors is that most of them are not going to go away. That's because stress is a natural part of life. It's *how we manage stress* that matters the most. Researchers have found that it is not so much a stressful *event* (such as an accident) that causes a strong emotional reaction like fear or depression as a person's coping or management skills that determine emotional health or breakdown.[14] It's *unmanaged or poorly managed stress* that is the enemy to marital satisfaction, not stress itself. Either you manage stress, or it manages you and your marriage.

Individuals who view the stressors in their life as unmanageable or overwhelming will develop such symptoms as anxiety, depression, stomach problems, sleep disturbances, and irritability. These reactions make you a difficult person to live with and also make you feel less good about your performance as a spouse. To manage stress, you must first feel that you have some control over things. You always have control over your attitude about life's stressors, and attitude is 90 percent of the solution. The other 10 percent is eliminating the stressors you can eliminate (for example, stop driving to work and take the bus), getting help managing stressors (ask a colleague to share some of your work with you), delegating work to others as you can (get a secretary or an assistant to work out the details on a project), and learning to say no more often to others' requests for your time and attention. It is beyond the scope of this book to teach you other stress management techniques (see Chapter Seven for a list of good sources), but if stress is negatively affecting your marriage, deal with it now. Sit down with your partner, and develop a stress management plan.

I recently counseled a couple to draw up such a plan, and here are some of the solutions they brought to the next therapy appointment:

1. The husband agreed to leave home thirty minutes earlier each morning to beat the traffic on the freeway. This made work go better, and he was less frazzled when he returned home at night.

2. The wife agreed to work no more than two hours overtime on any given day.

3. The couple organized their older children to do more of the housework before they got home from work. The kids started taking turns getting dinner started before their parents arrived home.

4. They lowered their expectations of the cleanliness level of the house at the end of the day. They discovered that a perfectly clean house wasn't as vital to their happiness as they originally thought. And on weekends, they cleaned more thoroughly with the children's help.

5. The husband agreed to say no to any more moonlighting job offers from friends. Although the extra income was nice, the toll on him and his marriage was not worth it.

Successfully implementing this plan proved to this couple that the stress in their marriage was largely under their control. As they executed the plan, their marriage improved.

🎰 Marriage Competitors: Work, Parenting, and Outside Interests

Time is a precious commodity—we only have so much each day. But why is it that the average American married couple spends only twenty to thirty minutes a day in meaningful conversation? Part of the problem is that we let work, parenting, and outside interests come before our marriage when planning and living our daily schedules. Part of the problem is that our time priorities are mixed up. Sometimes our affection priorities are, too. For example, who is the first person dad hugs when he gets through the door after work? Probably the children, the pet, and then his wife. We get so easily wrapped up in making a living, raising our children and giving them affection, and doing our hobbies and outside interests that after these, there is usually little or no time left for our marriage.

Some work schedules are incompatible with the kinds of companionship and intimacy we desire in marriage.[15] I remember a couple who complained of no sex life and marital doldrums. He had two jobs—during the day he was a firefighter, and at night he moonlighted as a security guard. She worked as a nurse all day and frequently picked up an additional shift or two during the week to help make financial ends meet. Since they worked so many hours and also had three children at home, any time spent at home was child-centered because they felt guilty about spending so much time away from the children. They even felt guilty leaving the children home with the oldest daughter as a babysitter so that they could go out for an evening alone together. There also was no time for personal outside interests (he said he used to like to play racquetball three times a week). For this couple, work and parenting had swallowed up their personal lives and with it their marriage.

In other marriages it is not so much the sheer number of hours worked that is the problem as the feeling that your spouse's work is more important to him emotionally and psychologically than you are.[16] The solution to these problems may involve minor or even drastic changes in your work schedules and boundaries (for example, not bringing work home with you) and giving couple time a higher priority.

Remember that children will consume all the time you give them and ask for more. It is your job to discern how much is enough and enforce the difference.[17] Parenting does not have to be a full-time, round-the-clock activity with service on demand. Sometimes simple solutions like putting the kids to bed one hour earlier are all it takes to enrich your marriage. Don't expect the children to like the change, but in doing so you are making a powerful statement about the value of your relationship. In some cases the children may even comment that they are happy to see Mom and Dad spending more time together alone each day. They intuitively know that their parents are easier people to deal with when they are happy with each other.

So you see that there *are* limits you can put on your work hours and parenting hours to gain some more time for your marriage. But what about individual outside pursuits that gobble up time you could be spending together? Hobbies, recreation, sports, television, and the Internet can consume couple time quickly. And how many times have you responded to a question from your spouse with, "Wait a second, I'm trying to hear the score of tonight's game!" or "Ask me that when I get off the computer"? These distractions are powerful absorbers of our time and attention. In themselves, none of them are evil; they just compete for couple time and attention.

You know you have a problem with too many outside interests or too much time spent in one of them when your partner refers to your behavior as if you are having an affair with it. You must learn to balance outside activities with couple activities. Unbalanced marriages do not survive year after year. And by the way, make sure your bedroom is media-free—no television, Internet, newspapers, magazines, or hobbies in that room. That room is reserved for couple connection through words or touch.[18]

✂ Scoring and Interpretation Guidelines

Here is the most important part of this chapter—evaluating and understanding your contexts test results. The scoring and interpretation guidelines follow the same order as the short tests you completed.

Fill out Worksheet 5.2 now so that you have your scores in front of you.

Trait	Range of Scores	Norm Score	Low Score	Your Score
Family of origin (items 1–4)	4–20	15	13	_____
Parental marriage satisfaction (items 5–7)	3–15	9	8	_____
Family process leftovers (items 8–10)	3–15	10	9	_____
Autonomy (items 11–12)	2–10	6	5	_____

Trait	Your Score
Parental conflict management style (item 13)	_____
Level of violence (item 14)	_____
Family sexual abuse (item 15)	_____
Outsider sexual abuse (item 16)	_____

Type of family (*write in family type from item 17*):

_____

Parents' and friends' approval (items 18–23):

Your father: _____   Partner's father: _____

Your mother: _____   Partner's mother: _____

Your friends: _____   Partner's friends: _____

Trait	Range of Scores	Norm Score	High Score	Your Score
Mother-in-law stress (items 24–26)	3–15	8	9	_____
Father-in-law stress (items 27–29)	3–15	8	9	_____
Perceived stress (items 30–32)	3–15	7	9	_____

Stress sources (*write the three current biggest stressors in your life from item 33*):

_____

_____

_____

Trait	Range of Scores	Norm Score	High Score	Your Score
Parenting stress (items 34–36)	3–15	8	10	_____
Work stress (items 37–39)	3–15	8	10	_____
Outside interests stress (items 40–42)	3–15	8	10	_____

Worksheet 5.2. Contexts Summary.

Family-of-Origin Effects

Look at your family-of-origin score on Worksheet 5.2. How healthy was your family of origin? (Scores at or above the norm are healthy.) Based on your score, is your family background a resource or liability in your marriage? In what ways? How has your experience in your family affected your ability to love and trust your spouse?

_____

_____

_____

_____

_____

Parents' Marriage

How happy was your parents' marriage? (Scores at or above the norm indicate that they were happily married.) How has their marriage served as a role model for your marriage? What marriage characteristics do they have that you want to follow? Avoid?

_____

_____

_____

_____

_____

Family Process Leftovers

How does your family process leftover score compare to the norm score? (Scores at or above the norm are high, meaning _fewer_ leftovers exist.) What problems from your past experiences in your family do you still need to overcome?

_____

_____

_____

_____

_____

Autonomy

How autonomous are you? (Scores at or above the norm reflect autonomy.) If applicable, what do you need to do to become more autonomous?

_____

_____

_____

_____

_____

Parents' Conflict Management Style

If your score is 3, 4, or 5, it means your parents handled conflict in a destructive manner, at least some of the time. This approach is referred to as a hostile conflict resolution style, which is known to be harmful to both individuals and to destroy marital satisfaction. If your parents used such a style, how did it affect you as a child? How does it affect how you resolve conflict with your spouse today?

_____

_____

_____

_____

_____

Impacts of Abuse

Items 14–16 refer to physical and sexual abuse that may have happened to you while growing up. If you scored any of these items 2, 3, 4, or 5, answer the following questions: How has the abuse affected you and your marriage? What can you do to get over the effects of the abuse? Who can help you with this?

_____

_____

_____

_____

_____

Family Structure

In what type of family did you spend most of your time growing up? How did growing up in this type of family situation affect your attitude about marriage and divorce? About commitment?

_____

_____

_____

_____

_____

Approval

Who approves the most of your marriage (the people you scored as 3 or 4)? Least (scored 1 or 2)? How is this approval or disapproval an asset or liability in your marriage? What can you do to increase the approval of people who disapprove of your relationship?

_____

_____

_____

_____

_____

In-Law Stress

How much stress is there currently in your relationship with your mother-in-law?
(Scores above the norm reflect a high level of stress.) Your father-in-law? What is the
cause of this stress? What can you do to lower the stress in these relationships? How
can your spouse help you?

_____

_____

_____

_____

_____

Perceived Stress

Overall, how stressed do you feel? (Scores of 9 or higher reflect high stress.) What are
the sources of stress in your life? What can you start doing to lower your feelings of
stress? Where can you get help?

_____

_____

_____

_____

_____

Stress Sources

What are your three biggest sources of stress today, and what can you do to lower the stress you feel concerning them? What can you do to improve the situation or make a positive difference? What can you do to let go of some of this stress? Who can help you?

_____

_____

_____

_____

Parenting Stress

The higher your score, the more likely you are neglecting your marriage in order to raise your children. You are giving away your married life to your kids. A score of 10 or higher suggests trouble. What can you do to set up better boundaries to get back a life with your mate?

_____

_____

_____

_____

_____

Work Stress

Scores of 10 or higher mean trouble here, too. Work is swallowing up your relationship. How can you set up better boundaries between work and marriage to give you more couple time and strengthen your relationship?

_____

_____

_____

_____

_____

Outside Interests

A score of 10 or higher means that outside interests are drowning your marriage. You have to make more time to be with your spouse or do more of these activities together so that they turn into couple activities. Which of your activities can you do together and enjoy? What *new* couple interests might you develop if you just took the time? What individual outside activities do you need to cut back on?

_____

_____

_____

_____

_____

🔵 Your Big Picture

Finally, based on all of the contexts assessments and written responses, list your *contexts* that are assets and liabilities for your marriage:

Assets   *Liabilities*

_____   _____

_____   _____

_____   _____

_____   _____

_____   _____
_____   _____
_____   _____
_____   _____

You have now finished assessing the third and final factor in the Marriage Triangle—your contexts. In the next chapter you will summarize all your findings and insights from the three dimensions of the triangle and be in a better position to answer some very important questions: Overall, what assets and liabilities are in your marriage today? What are your goals and plans for improvement? Exciting answers await you in Chapter Six.

Your Own Personal Marriage Triangle

Putting the Three Factors Together

This will be the most interesting and most important chapter of this book for you because first I will summarize all you have learned about the three factors in the Marriage Triangle. Then I will help you summarize all you have learned about yourself and your relationship in the short tests in Chapters Three through Five on the your own personal Marriage Triangle Summary Sheet. It will help you organize and analyze your results and set goals for improvement in your marriage. By knowing what your Marriage Triangle contains, you can take the first step in avoiding its becoming the "Bermuda Triangle of marriage"!

First, look back at Figure 2.1, which identifies all the factors that predict marital satisfaction. While some of these factors are assets or strengths in your marriage (for example, high self-esteem, good couple communication skills, and good in-law relationships) and promote marital satisfaction, others are liabilities or weaknesses (anger, criticism, too much career stress) that diminish marital satisfaction. The greater your ratio of assets to liabilities, the higher your marital satisfaction.

First, let's look at two examples of how to use the summary sheet; then we'll look at two action plans for tuning up a marriage.

Using the Summary Sheet

David and Francine

Figure 6.1 shows the results for David (forty-nine) and Francine (forty-eight) after they prepared a plan for strengthening their marriage. The assets and liabilities listed came from their liabilities and strengths summaries at the end of Chapters Three, Four, and Five.

This couple had been married twenty-four years and had three children, aged twenty-one, sixteen, and fourteen. David was a customer service analyst who had recently been promoted to vice president in his organization. Francine was a professor at a local college. Assets or strengths included overall good emotional health for both spouses. The

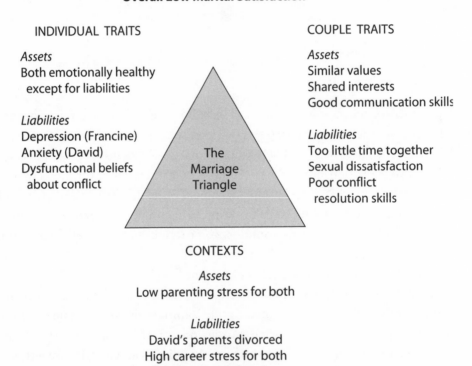

Overall Low Marital Satisfaction

INDIVIDUAL TRAITS

Assets
Both emotionally healthy
  except for liabilities

Liabilities
Depression (Francine)
Anxiety (David)
Dysfunctional beliefs
  about conflict

COUPLE TRAITS

Assets
Similar values
Shared interests
Good communication skills

Liabilities
Too little time together
Sexual dissatisfaction
Poor conflict
  resolution skills

The
Marriage
Triangle

CONTEXTS

Assets
Low parenting stress for both

Liabilities
David's parents divorced
High career stress for both
High perceived stress
Stressors: retirement planning, debt, college expenses
Parental disapproval

Figure 6.1. David and Francine's Marriage Triangle Summary Sheet.

only exception was some moderate depression for Francine and anxiety for David. These two problems were related to their contexts in these ways: David was relatively new in his vice president position and anxious about how he would perform in that that role. He was not used to being a leader. He rated his self-esteem as low, too. Francine was feeling job burnout in her career with no plan for resolving it soon and few perceived options for other employment. Both of them were overworking—David brought home paperwork to do five nights a week, and Francine graded papers three nights a week at her office. They often felt their lives were out of control or too complicated.

Other life stressors included retirement-planning stress for both of them (they wanted to retire in twelve years), paying for the children's college tuition and car insurance, and debt problems. Fortunately, at this time in their family's developmental cycle, parenting stress (such as discipline) was lower than when the children were younger, and the couple could easily go out together on weekends without worrying about child care. Another asset was their many mutual interests—they enjoyed golf, skiing, racquetball, music, and the theater together. The problem was finding time and money to do these things. They had not been out alone together for nearly two months, and the last trip they took alone was two years earlier. They both reported sexual dissatisfaction, which was related to depression, anxiety, stress, and overwork.

A major family-of-origin issue from David's past became more relevant to his marriage now than it ever had before. His parents divorced when he was sixteen years old—his father had an affair, and his mother divorced him as a result. He never saw his parents resolve conflict productively; instead, they ignored conflict and stress and eventually emotionally grew apart. Although David's communication skills were rated as above average, his preferred conflict resolution style was like his parents': conflict-phobic. Rather than discussing their poor sex life, debts, and stress levels with Francine, they ignored these important topics, unrealistically believing that they would solve themselves over time. Like his father, David was afraid of conflict. David's parents were still bitter about their divorce and did little to encourage David and Francine to strengthen their own marriage. In fact, both parents disapproved of the marriage from the beginning. In the back of his mind David knew that if things got too bad between him and Francine, he could follow his father's example—in other words, he knew that divorce was an option. To his credit, though, he was still committed to Francine and the marriage when he completed this assessment.

David and Francine's marriage tune-up plan is shown in Exhibit 6.1. The plan was successfully implemented over a five-month period, resulting in improvement in all areas, especially in overall marital satisfaction.

Overall Tune-Up Goals

Improve stress management and conflict resolution skills; eliminate negative beliefs and influences from the past.

Specific Areas to Tune Up

1. Lower anxiety (David) and improve mood and self-esteem (Francine).

2. Eliminate dysfunctional beliefs.

3. Improve conflict resolution skills.

4. Spend more quality time together.

5. Improve sexual satisfaction.

6. Deal with stress more effectively—get control.

7. Eliminate negativity about marriage from past (David).

8. Deal better with parental disapproval.

9. Develop plans for dealing with major stressors.

Tune-Up Plans

1. We will complete individual therapy to overcome depression, anxiety, dysfunctional beliefs, and negative attitudes about marriage.

2. We will enroll in a stress management program at David's company-sponsored employee assistance program to learn to deal better with stress.

3. We will develop a detailed financial plan for covering college costs.

4. We will attend a retirement-planning seminar.

5. We will complete a couple communication workshop to learn better conflict management skills and stop ignoring conflict.

6. We will use a weekly planner to designate a date night every week and a weekend romantic getaway at least once every sixty days.

7. We will limit the number of nights we bring work home to two nights a week. At least one night a week, we will do an activity together or watch a movie alone.

8. We will set limits with David's parents on how much feedback and suggestions they make concerning our marriage.

Exhibit 6.1. David and Francine's Marriage Tune-Up Plan.

Ross and Jenny

A second example involves a couple at a different stage in the family life cycle. Ross and Jenny (both thirty) had been married five years and were both in the fourth year of their first jobs. Ross was a pilot for the national forest service, and Jenny was a book-keeper for a ranch and farm supply dealer. They had two young children, aged three and one. Their marital assets and liabilities reflected both their stage in the family life cycle and their own idiosyncrasies as individuals and as a couple (see Figure 6.2).

Assets that stood out in this relatively young marriage were high levels of love and commitment, sexual satisfaction, consensus on major values, career satisfaction for both individuals, and happily married parents on both sides of the family.

Overall Moderate Marital Satisfaction

INDIVIDUAL TRAITS

Assets
Love
Commitment

Liabilities
Nonassertiveness (Ross)
Anger and hostility (Jenny)

COUPLE TRAITS

Assets
Sexual satisfaction
Consensus

Liabilities
Poor communication skills
Poor conflict resolution skills
Lack of affection

The Marriage Triangle

CONTEXTS

Assets
Career satisfaction
Happily married parents

Liabilities
Dysfunctional family of origin (Ross)
In-law conflicts
Parenting stress

Figure 6.2. Ross and Jenny's Marriage Triangle Summary Sheet.

Liabilities uncovered included Ross's nonassertiveness and Jenny's anger, which frequently led to hostility when they discussed important issues, along with poor communication skills (poor listening skills and frequent interruptions during discussions by both spouses), a hostile conflict resolution style, and a lack of nonsexual affection. They came to see me for these problems plus three issues from the contexts of their marriage: Ross grew up in a highly dysfunctional family that was emotionally cold and detached. He seldom experienced any kind of affection or validation from his parents. This was related to his struggle to show his wife, Jenny, nonsexual affection in their marriage relationship. In addition, Jenny had a conflictual relationship with Ross's parents—she felt that she could never make them happy, that they were jealous of the time Ross spent with her, and that they resented the couple's decision not to attend every family event that occurred (they lived four hundred miles apart). Ross's parents blamed Jenny for this decision. Finally, as often happens with new parents, they spent too much time parenting and not enough time together alone. This problem was vividly expressed when they came to their first therapy session accompanied by both children! In our second session (without the children), they reported that this was the first hour they had spent alone away from the children in over a month!

As a result of their Marriage Triangle assessment, they devised the marriage tune-up plan in Exhibit 6.2. It only took them three months to carry out this plan. It is interesting to note that their new plan for the in-laws actually involved *more* contact with Ross's parents than before, after a long telephone conversation between Jenny and his parents to clarify viewpoints and resolve hurt feelings from the past on both sides. It was especially gratifying to see Ross learn how to be more affectionate with Jenny. These two solutions (regarding the in-laws and affection) greatly reduced Jenny's anger. And I was very impressed with the couple's ability to begin using new communication skills after reading a book I recommended.

Completing Your Own Summary Sheet

Now it's time for you to develop your own Marriage Triangle Summary Sheet. Follow these steps:

1. In the spaces provided in Figure 6.3, list your assets and liabilities from the summary pages in Chapters Three, Four, and Five.

Overall Tune-Up Goal

Improve communication and conflict resolution skills so as to deal with other issues.

Specific Areas to Tune Up

1. Improve communication, assertiveness, and conflict resolution skills.

2. Deal with anger more appropriately.

3. Be more affectionate.

4. Reduce conflicts and hurt feelings with in-laws.

5. Make more time for couple activities alone.

Tune-Up Plans

1. We will complete marital therapy to improve our communication skills and change our conflict resolution style.

2. We will read self-help books on anger management, assertiveness, and being more affectionate and will employ the techniques taught in them with the therapist's assistance.

3. We will devise a new plan for how often we visit his parents and how to deal better with their criticism or disappointment.

4. We will schedule at least one night of the week for a date and develop a list of child care providers we trust and can afford.

Exhibit 6.2. Ross and Jenny's Marriage Tune-Up Plan.

2. List the areas to strengthen on Worksheet 6.1. Be specific.

3. List plans laying out how you will strengthen each of these areas. Be specific. (Specific resources you can draw on are found in Chapter Seven.)

Figure 6.3. Your Marriage Triangle Summary Sheet.

What are the best solutions for strengthening areas that need improvement? For example, self-help books are useful in some areas (see Chapter Seven). Counseling with a trusted friend or clergy person works better for more difficult problems (for example, individual problems and couple problems). Professional therapy is usually necessary for more chronic and serious individual and couple problems (for example, depression and destructive conflict resolution styles). Professional therapy is

Overall Tune-Up Goal

_____

Specific Areas to Tune Up

1. _____

   _____

2. _____

   _____

3. _____

   _____

4. _____

   _____

5. _____

   _____

Tune-Up Plans

1. _____

   _____

2. _____

   _____

3. _____

   _____

4. _____

   _____

5. _____

   _____

Worksheet 6.1. Your Marriage Tune-Up Plan.

strongly recommended for problems such as alcoholism or drug dependency and for overcoming the negative effects of physical or sexual abuse. The same applies for overcoming the negative effects of infidelity. Finally, skills development programs are very useful when trying to improve such skills as empathic listening, assertiveness, and conflict resolution techniques. More details on these types of skills development programs are described in Chapter Seven.

CHAPTER
SEVEN 𝔤

Additional Resources for Marriage Tune-Ups

Now that you have assessed your marriage and set goals, I hope you are more interested in learning about other resources that will help you tune up your relationship. The resources described in this chapter include books, courses, programs, and organizations. They are organized, like the rest of this book, according to the three dimensions of the Marriage Triangle.

𝔤 Individual Traits Resources

This section contains recommended resources for building self-esteem, overcoming neurotic traits—especially anxiety, depression, and anger—and changing dysfunctional beliefs about relationships and marriage.

Feeling Good: The New Mood Therapy by David Burns (New York: Avon Books. 1999). This best-seller deserves the acclaim it has received. It explains how depression, anxiety, anger, and low self-esteem develop and are effectively treated using Burns's scientifically tested method of cognitive therapy and coping skills. I have recommended this book to more clients than any other. One of my favorite chapters is titled "Dare to Be Average! Ways to Overcome Perfectionism." Burns shows you step by step how to overcome emotional problems. His chapter on psychotropic drugs used to treat depression and anxiety is also very informative. The power of this book is that it can be effectively used to treat all six neurotic traits that predict marital dissatisfaction.

Your Perfect Right: A Guide to Assertive Living by Robert Alberti and Michael Emmons (San Luis Obispo, Calif.: Impact, 1990). Another well-deserved best-seller. Learn why you lack assertiveness and how to become more assertive (not aggressive) with others. This includes honest self-expression and directness without hurting others or feeling guilty about it.

Anger: The Misunderstood Emotion by Carol Tavris (New York: Touchstone Books, 1989). This book deals with popular myths about anger, such as "Expressing your anger reduces anger and makes you feel better." Tavris shows you how to develop more functional ways of controlling your anger and dealing with it when it occurs.

A New Guide to Rational Living by Albert Ellis and Robert Harper (Upper Saddle River, N.J.: Prentice Hall, 1975). A classic, like Burns's book, in overcoming dysfunctional beliefs (Ellis calls them "irrational beliefs") and developing more functional or rational beliefs by restructuring your thinking in ways that will lead to more personal and relationship satisfaction.

Why Love Is Not Enough by Sol Gordon (Boston: Bob Adams, 1988). This book will help you dispel myths about marriage and show you a more realistic look at what makes marriage work—it does take more than love. (You know that now, right?) It's a very provocative and useful book.

The Truth About Love by Patricia Love (New York: Fireside Books, 2001). An interesting and useful look at how love develops and changes over the course of marriage, the role of friendship in marriage, and how to rekindle love (a *very* popular chapter!). This book explains the different types of love better than any other source I've seen and helps normalize the highs and lows we all experience in marriage. Most important, it gives direction on how to build commitment and a lasting love.

🙿 Couple Traits Resources

I emphasized earlier that communication and conflict resolution skills are among the best predictors of marital satisfaction. You can improve your skills by reading and practicing the principles in books I list here or by participating in a communication skills training program at your local college, church, synagogue, YMCA, or YWCA. Most important, I list programs with scientific support for their validity. In addition,

I list some of the best overall marriage enrichment books and programs I have studied. Let's start with communication skills training books and programs.

The *Prevention and Relationship Enhancement Program (PREP)* is based on twenty years of research, which has shown that couples who successfully participate in this six-week program have lower rates of breakup and divorce and report more satisfying relationships, fewer negative communication patterns, and higher levels of positive communication as a result of the program. PREP is traditionally offered in weekend workshops or in six weekly session of two hours each. For more information about the program, contact PREP, Inc., P.O. Box 102530, Denver, CO 80250; (303) 759-9931; www.PREPinc.com. The PREP office can also send you a list of audiotapes and videotapes that focus on helping couples preserve and enhance their marriages by teaching communication and conflict resolution skills, deepening love, friendship, fun, sensuality, and commitment.

Fighting for *Your Marriage: Positive Steps for Preventing Divorce and Preserving a Lasting Love* by Howard Markman, Scott Stanley, and Susan L. Blumberg (San Francisco: Jossey-Bass, 2001) contains the content of the PREP program. Order it to get a start on the program on your own.

The *Couple Communication Program (CC) (I & II)* has been studied for more than thirty years and has resulted in dozens of research studies showing its effectiveness in improving couple's speaking, listening, and conflict resolution skills and overall marital satisfaction. You can complete CC in a group with an instructor and six to twelve other couples (totaling eight hours) or by yourselves as a couple with an instructor in six fifty-minute sessions. For information on CC programs in your community contact Interpersonal Communication Programs, 30752 Southview Drive, Suite 200, Evergreen, CO 80439; (800) 328-5099; www.couplecommunication.com.

Another research-based communication skills training program is called *Relationship Enhancement (RE)*. Couples learn speaking, listening, conflict resolution, self-change, helping the other change, and other skills during this workshop. The RE program most recently developed a home study version wherein couples get four hours of private coaching from a trained coach on the telephone. It is referred to as PhoneCoach. RE is a very effective program, and I recommend it. For more information about skills training and marriage enrichment weekends, contact the National Institute of Relationship Enhancement, 4400 East-West Highway, Suite 28, Bethesda, MD 20814; (800) 4-FAMILIES; www.nire.org.

Another relationship skills course is called *PAIRS* (Practical Application of Intimate Relationship Skills). It is a four- to five-month, 120-hour course focused on communication skills, conflict resolution skills, understanding self and others, and the logic of love and emotions. For more information about this program, contact: PAIRS International, Inc., 9400 North Central Expressway, Suite 310, Dallas, TX 75231; (888) PAIRS-4U; www.pairs.com.

Excellent books focused on improving couple dynamics include the following:

Hot Monogamy: Essential Steps to More Passionate, Intimate Lovemaking by Patricia Love and Jo Robinson (New York: Plume Books, 1995). A great book on how to improve sexual functioning and satisfaction. Especially useful for couples where one's sex drive is stronger than the other's.

The Act of Marriage by Tim and Beverly LaHaye (Grand Rapids, Mich.: Zondervan, 1998) is a classic "marriage sex manual" including important chapters on male and female differences, the beauty of sex in marriage, and the art of lovemaking. This is a book that *all* couples should read *before* they get married as well as after! Very helpful and tasteful.

Divorce Busting by Michele Weiner-Davis (New York: Fireside Books, 1993) is a classic on how to improve your marriage even if you have to do it without much help from your spouse. It provides simple but effective strategies for improving your marriage and interrupting destructive patterns using creative and positive changes in your own behavior. The book is very optimistic and solution-focused rather than problem-focused.

Why Marriages Succeed or Fail by John Gottman (New York: Fireside Books, 1994) describes in detail how to overcome destructive conflict resolution styles and negative thinking patterns in marriage. It also has an excellent chapter on male and female differences in communication styles that will help you understand yourself and your partner better. The three styles of conflict resolution that work and the one that leads to divorce are important for all couples to understand.

Finally, here is a book about self-help books, Internet sites, and movies:

Authoritative Guide to Self-Help Resources in Mental Health by John Norcress, John Santrock, Linda Campbell, Thomas Smith, Robert Sommer, and Edward Zuckerman (New York: Guilford Press, 2000). This book is a gold mine of information on hundreds of topics from depression to sex to marriage to parenting. Resources are not just listed but also rated for quality and helpfulness based on national studies of therapists who recommend books to their clients.

❧ Context Resources

These resources focus on the third dimension of the Marriage Triangle—contexts. Resources described here can help you overcome family-of-origin experiences that continue to affect you in negative ways today and can assist you in dealing with problems with your parents and friends in a healthier and more direct way. Resources for stress management are also listed.

How to Deal with Your Parents by Lynn Osterkamp (New York: Berkley Books, 1992). This book will help you communicate more effectively with your family and get along with them more smoothly. The author helps you set goals for improving relationships and then helps you develop a plan to meet your goals. She also deals with issues such as coping with controlling parents, dealing with disapproval, becoming more autonomous, and avoiding being manipulated.

Right to Innocence: Healing the Trauma of Childhood Sexual Abuse by Beverly Engle (New York: Ivy Books, 1990). This is a classic on how women can overcome the trauma of childhood sexual abuse and change their identity from "victim" to "survivor." It includes step-by-step directions on how to forgive, heal, and go on with your life. It also contains guidelines for parents and friends who can support you.

Victims No Longer: Men Recovering from Incest and Other Childhood Sexual Abuse by Michael Lew (New York: Harper Perennial, 1990). Like *Right to Innocence,* this book helps readers, this time men, overcome the negative effects of sexual abuse on themselves and on their adult relationships.

It Will Never Happen to Me by Claudia Black (New York: Ballantine Books, 1981). Another classic—this time the focus is on assessing the effects of growing up with an alcoholic parent. Black stresses recovering from negative emotional effects and leads the reader through the recovery process.

Willpower's Not Enough: Recovering from Addictions of Every Kind by Arnold Washton and Donna Boundy (New York: Harper Perennial, 1989). Of all the books I have read, this is the best when it comes to explaining to the lay reader how addictions of all kinds may develop and are treated. It's a great book for people seeking to understand their addict or themselves. It includes a powerful step-by-step procedure for recovering from addictions of all kinds—alcohol, drugs, sex, gambling, spending, eating, exercise, or whatever.

The Relaxation and Stress Reduction Workbook by Martha Davis, Elizabeth Eschelman, and Matthew McKay (Oakland, Calif.: New Harbinger, 1995). Use this book to learn how to better understand your personal reactions to stress and how to relax and manage stress in a number of environmental settings.

Take Back Your Marriage by William Doherty (New York: Guilford Press, 2001). This is a great book that focuses on three major stressors that can negatively affect marriage—parenting stress, career stress, and outside interest influences. Practical solutions to these problems are given. Interesting chapters on resisting family and friends who would undermine your marriage, resisting marital therapists who may threaten your marriage, and developing love rituals in your relationship are included. Also see the chapter on how to select a qualified marital therapist.

℅ Organizations for Marriage Enrichment

To get more information on preparing for marriage and enriching marriage, contact a relatively new organization, the *Coalition for Marriage, Family, and Couples Education (CMFCE)*. This organization's goal is "to increase the availability of skill-based marriage education courses in the community." The CMFCE network disseminates detailed information about many marriage education programs, books, videos, audiotapes, therapy resources, and workshops around the country. And it has a useful and informative electronic newsletter that publishes marriage-related information on a daily basis. It is a marriage enrichment gold mine! You may contact the CMFCE at 5310 Belt Road, N.W., Washington, DC 20015; (202) 362-3332; www.smartmarriages.com.

Two comprehensive marriage assessment questionnaires are also available at a relatively low cost ($10 to $30 per couple):

RELATionship Evaluation (RELATE) ($10 per couple) is a 271-item questionnaire that can be taken by unmarried and married couples on the Internet. Many of the items in this book came from the RELATE questionnaire. However, taking RELATE is a quick, inexpensive, and informative way to evaluate your relationship. You and your partner receive a nineteen-page self-interpretive report to study on your own or with a therapist's assistance. RELATE is the most accessible, least expensive, and most comprehensive assessment questionnaire on the market. And you can take RELATE several times over the course of your relationship to get a quick picture of the condition of your marriage. Remarriage assessment items are included, too.

RELATE is available in English, Spanish, and Portuguese. To take RELATE, contact the RELATE Institute, Family Studies Center, 350 SWKT, Brigham Young University, Provo, UT 84602; (801) 378-4359; www.relate.byu.edu.

A second marriage assessment questionnaire I highly recommend is called *Enriching Relationship Issues, Communication, and Happiness (ENRICH)* ($30 per couple, 165 items). Two versions are available: *ENRICH* for married couples and *Mature Age Transitional Evaluation (MATE)* for couples over fifty years old. MATE is used for enrichment purposes as well as to help older couples going through a transition like retirement or relocation. Both questionnaires are used only with the assistance of a counselor who has been trained in using these inventories. Excellent follow-up materials are included to make the results more meaningful to the couple. For more information on these questionnaires, contact Life Innovations, Inc., P.O. Box 190, Minneapolis, MN 55440; (800) 331-1661; www.lifeinnovations.com.

If you need a referral for individual or marital therapy, contact the American Association for Marriage and Family Therapy (AAMFT), 1133 Fifteenth Street, N.W., Suite 300, Washington, DC 20005; (202) 452-0109; www.aamft.org. The AAMFT maintains a national directory of qualified marital therapists.

How to Find a Competent Therapist

Regardless of the type of therapist you see (psychologist, marriage and family therapist, professional counselor, social worker, or pastoral counselor), be sure he or she is licensed in your state and has specialized training in marital therapy approaches. Not all therapists have this specialized training. And note that psychiatrists, who are usually the professionals most people first think of going to when they have problems, do not do marital therapy. Instead, they refer couples to one of the other mental health professions—usually, marital therapists.

Here are the questions you should ask the therapist before your first marital therapy session:

1. What is your training background in marital therapy?

2. What is your opinion about divorce? Do you ever recommend divorce? Why?

3. What percentage of couples you have counseled have reported an improvement in their marriage as a result of your therapy with them?

4. What do you believe about gender differences in marriage? How do you use these beliefs in helping couples?

5. What do you do if a couple starts an angry exchange during a session? (A good answer is that the therapist interrupts and helps the couple deal with the issue more calmly.)

6. What specialized training do you have in teaching couples communication and conflict resolution skills?

7. In the absence of abuse or danger, will you support the possibility that we can salvage our marriage?[1]

Notes

Chapter One Overcoming Myths About Marriage

1. W. J. Lederer and D. D. Jackson, *The Mirages of Marriage* (New York: Norton, 1968), p. 55.

2. M. S. Peck, *The Road Less Traveled: A New Psychology of Love, Traditional Values, and Spiritual Growth* (New York: Simon & Schuster, 1978), p. 85.

3. H. S. Sullivan, *Conceptions of Modern Psychiatry* (New York: Norton, 1953), pp. 42–43.

4. Myths 1, 2, 4, and 6 from N. S. Jacobson and G. Margolin, *Marital Therapy* (New York: Brunner/Mazel, 1979); remainder from A. A. Lazarus, *Marital Myths* (San Luis Obispo, Calif.: Impact, 1985).

5. J. Gottman, *Why Marriages Succeed or Fail* (New York: Simon & Schuster, 1994). Excerpt reprinted with the permission of Simon & Schuster; copyright © 1994 by John Gottman.

6. Jacobson and Margolin, *Marital Therapy,* p. 148.

7. Jacobson and Margolin, *Marital Therapy.*

8. D. Mace, "Marriage and Family Enrichment: A New Field?" *Family Relations,* 1979, *28,* 409–419.

9. Mace, "Marriage and Family Enrichment."

10. Mace, "Marriage and Family Enrichment."

Chapter Two The Marriage Triangle

1. T. B. Holman, D. M. Busby, C. Doxey, D. M. Klein, and V. Loyer-Carlson, *RELATionship Evaluation (RELATE)* (Provo, Utah: RELATE Institute, 1997).

2. T. B. Holman and Associates, *Premarital Prediction of Marital Quality or Breakup: Research, Theory, and Practice* (New York: Kluwer/Plenum, 2001).

3. D. M. Busby, T. B. Holman, and N. Taniguchi, "RELATE: Relationship Evaluation of the Individual, Family, Cultural, and Couple Contexts." *Family Relations,* 2001, *50,* 308–316.

4. J. H. Larson and T. B. Holman, "Premarital Predictors of Marital Quality and Stability," *Family Relations,* 1994, *43,* 228–237; Holman and Associates, *Premarital Predictors of Marital Quality or Breakup;* T. N. Bradbury, "Assessing the Four Fundamental Domains of Marriage," *Family Relations,* 1995, *44,* 459–468; B. R. Karney and T. N. Bradbury, "The Longitudinal Course of Marital Quality and Stability: A Review of Theory, Methods, and Research," *Psychological Bulletin,* 1995, *18,* 3–34.

5. Unless otherwise indicated, all worksheet items in this book are from T. B. Holman, D. M. Busby, C. Doxey, D. M. Klein, and V. Loyer-Carlson, *RELATionship Evaluation (RELATE).* Used with permission from the RELATE Institute. Copyright © 1997, RELATE Institute, Provo, Utah.

6. B. Barlow, *Twelve Traps in Today's Marriage* (Salt Lake City, Utah: Deseret, 1986).

7. Lederer and Jackson, *Mirages of Marriage,* p. 17.

8. C. Doxey and J. H. Larson, *The RELATE Report* (Provo, Utah: RELATE Institute, 1997).

9. J. H. Larson, *Should We Stay Together? A Scientifically Proven Method for Evaluating Your Relationship and Improving Its Chances for Long-Term Success* (San Francisco: Jossey-Bass, 2000), fig. 2.2. Reprinted by permission of John Wiley & Sons, Inc.

Chapter Three   Factor 1: Your Individual Traits

1. L. A. Kurdek, "Predicting Marital Dissolution: A Five-Year Prospective Longitudinal Study of Newly Wed Couples," *Journal of Personality and Social Psychology,* 1993, *64,* 221–242.

2. Items 33–35 are from Z. Rubin, "Measurement of Romantic Love," *Journal of Personality and Social Psychology,* 1970, *16,* 265–273; used with permission. Items 36–38 are from S. M. Stanley and H. J. Markman, "Assessing Commitment in Personal Relationships," *Journal of Marriage and Family,* 1992, *54,* 595–608; used with permission from the National Council on Family Relations; copyright © 1992. Items 41–55 are from D. Baucom and N. Epstein, *Cognitive-Behavioral Marital Therapy* (New York: Taylor & Francis, 1990); copyright © 1990 by Taylor & Francis Publications; used with permission.

3. R. R. McCrae and P. T. Costa, *Personality in Adulthood* (New York: Guilford Press, 1990).

4. L. M. Wright, W. L. Watson, and J. M. Bell, *Beliefs: The Heart of Healing Families and Illness* (New York: Basic Books, 1996), p. 5.

5. Baucom and Epstein, *Cognitive Behavioral Marital Therapy,* pp. 442–444.

6. D. J. Canary and T. M. Emmers-Sommer, *Sex and Gender Differences in Personal Relationships* (New York: Guilford Press, 1997).

7. M. Weiner-Davis, *Divorce Busting* (New York: Fireside Books, 1993), p. 63.

8. C. Jamison and F. Scogin, "The Outcome of Cognitive Bibliotherapy with Depressed Adults," *Journal of Consulting and Clinical Psychology,* 1995, *63,* 644–650. A. E. Finch, M. J. Lambert, and G. Brown, "Attacking Anxiety: A Naturalistic Study of a Multimedia Self-Help Program," *Journal of Clinical Psychology,* 2000, *56,* 11–21.

9. Weiner-Davis, *Divorce Busting.*

10. Stanley and Markman, "Assessing Commitment in Personal Relationships."

11. Larson, *Should We Stay Together?*

12. Gottman, *Why Marriages Succeed or Fail.*

13. H. Markman, S. Stanley, and S. L. Blumberg, *Fighting for Your Marriage: Positive Steps for Preventing Divorce and Preserving a Lasting Love,* 2nd ed. (San Francisco: Jossey-Bass, 2001).

Chapter Four   Factor 2: Your Couple Traits

1. Gottman, *Why Marriages Succeed or Fail.*

2. Larson, *Should We Stay Together?*

3. H. Joanning, J. Brewster, and J. Koval, "The Communication Rapid Assessment Scale: Development of a Behavioral Index of Communication Quality," *Journal of Marital and Family Therapy,* 1984, *10,* 409–417.

4. Items 13–24 from C. E. Rusbult, D. J. Johnson, and G. D. Morrow, "Impact of Couple Patterns of Problem Solving on Distress and Nondistress in Dating Relationships," *Journal of Personality and Social Psychology,* 1986, *50,* 744–753. Used with permission of C. E. Rusbult and the American Psychological Association. Copyright © 1986 by the American Psychological Association. Items 25–39 from Gottman, *Why Marriages Succeed or Fail.* Copyright © 1994 by John Gottman. Used with permission of Simon & Schuster. Items 42–44 from E. M. Waring, "The Measurement of Marital Intimacy," *Journal of Marital and Family Therapy,* 1984, *10,* 185–192. Used with permission of E. M. Waring. Items 45–47 from W. W. Hudson, D. F. Harrison, and P. C. Crosscup, "A Short-Term Scale to Measure Sexual Discord in Dyadic Relationships," *Journal of Sex Research,* 1981, *17,* 157–174. Used with permission of the *Journal of Sex Research* and the Society for the Scientific Study of Sexuality. Copyright © 1981 by the Society for the Scientific Study of Sexuality. Items 46–51 from D. Busby, C. Christensen, D. R. Crane, and J. H. Larson, "A Revision of the Dyadic Adjustment Scale for Use with Distressed and Nondistressed Couples: Construct Hierarchy and Multidimensional Scales," *Journal of Marital and Family Therapy,* 1995, *21,* 289–308. Used with permission of D. Busby and the American Association for Marriage and Family Therapy. Copyright © 1995 by the American Association for Marriage and Family Therapy. Items 54–56 from D. H. Olson and J. Tiesel, *FACES II: Linear Scoring and Interpretation* (St. Paul: University of Minnesota, Family Social Science, 1991). Used with permission of D. Olson. Items 60–62 from W. R. Schumm, E. D. Scanlon, C. L. Crow, D. J. Green, and D. L. Buckler, "Characteristics of the Kansas Marital Satisfaction Scale in a Sample of 79 Married Couples," *Psychological Reports,* 1983, *53,* 583–588. Used with permission of the authors and the publisher. Items 63–65 from M. T. Schaefer and D. H. Olson, "Assessing Intimacy: The Pair Inventory," *Journal of Marital and Family Therapy,* 1981, *7,* 47–60. Used with permission of the authors and the American Association for Marriage and Family Therapy. Copyright © 1981 by the American Association for Marriage and Family Therapy.

5. S. L. Miller, E. W. Nunnally, D. B. Wackman, and P. A. Miller, *Talking and Listening Together* (Evergreen, Colo.: Interpersonal Communication Programs, 1991).

6. Miller, Nunnally, Wackman, and Miller, *Talking and Listening Together.*

7. Joanning, Brewster, and Koval, "The Communication Rapid Assessment Scale."

8. C. E. Rusbult and I. M. Zembrodt, "Responses to Dissatisfaction in Romantic Involvements: A Multidimensional Scaling Analysis," *Journal of Experimental Social Psychology,* 1983, *19,* 277.

9. Rusbult, Johnson, and Morrow, "Impact of Couple Patterns."

10. Gottman, *Why Marriages Succeed or Fail.*

11. Gottman, *Why Marriages Succeed or Fail.*

12. P. McGraw, "Bourgeois Marriage," *Smart Marriages Newsletter,* Mar. 2000, p. 5.

Chapter Five   Factor 3: Your Personal and Relationship Contexts

1. Items 24–29 from C. M. Bryant, R. D. Conger, and J. M. Mechum, "The Influence of In-Laws on Change in Marital Success," *Journal of Marriage and Family,* 2001, *63,* 614–626. Copyright © 2001 by the National Council on Family Relations. Used with permission. Items 30–32 from S. Cohen, T. Kamarck, and R. Mermelstein, "A Global Measure of Perceived Stress," *Journal of Health and Social Behavior,* 1983, *24,* 385–396. Used with permission of the American Psychological Association.

2. Gottman, *Why Marriages Succeed or Fail.*

3. P. R. Amato, "Explaining the Intergenerational Transmission of Divorce," *Journal of Marriage and Family,* 1996, *58,* 628–640.

4. Amato, "Explaining the Intergenerational Transmission of Divorce."

5. Amato, "Explaining the Intergenerational Transmission of Divorce."
6. Larson, *Should We Stay Together?*
7. Larson, *Should We Stay Together?*
8. Larson, *Should We Stay Together?*
9. N. Warren, *Finding the Love of Your Life* (Colorado Springs, Colo.: Focus on the Family, 1992).
10. Bryant, Conger, and Mechum, "Influence of In-Laws."
11. L. Berg-Cross, *Couples Therapy* (Thousand Oaks, Calif.: Sage, 1997).
12. W. Doherty, *Take Back Your Marriage* (New York: Guilford Press, 2001).
13. Doherty, *Take Back Your Marriage.*
14. Cohen, Kamarck, and Mermelstein, "Global Measure of Perceived Stress."
15. Doherty, *Take Back Your Marriage.*
16. Doherty, *Take Back Your Marriage.*
17. Doherty, *Take Back Your Marriage.*
18. Doherty, *Take Back Your Marriage.*

Chapter Seven   Additional Resources for Marriage Tune-Ups

1. Doherty, *Take Back Your Marriage.*

The Author

Jeffry H. Larson is a professor and former department chairman of the Department of Marriage and Family Therapy in the School of Family Life at Brigham Young University in Provo, Utah. He holds a bachelor of science degree (1971) and a master of science degree (1974) in psychology from Brigham Young University and a doctorate in marriage and family therapy from Texas Tech University (1980). Larson has more than two decades of experience conducting premarital counseling and marriage therapy and has taught marriage preparation, marriage enhancement, and marital therapy courses at four major universities. His research has focused on premarital predictors of marital satisfaction, the assessment of readiness for marriage, and the development of marriage education programs. He has published more than fifty articles in major professional journals and is coauthor (with Tom Holman) of an academic book on premarital prediction research, *Premarital Prediction of Marital Quality or Breakup* (Plenum, 2001). He is also author of the best-selling book *Should We Stay Together? A Scientifically Proven Method for Evaluating Your Relationship and Improving Its Chances for Long-Term Success* (Jossey-Bass, 2000).

Larson served as chairperson of the Marriage Preparation Focus Group of the National Council on Family Relations and is a licensed marriage and family therapist (LMFT) and a certified family life educator (CFLE). In addition, he is a clinical member and approved supervisor in the American Association for Marriage and Family Therapy and serves as a member of the Utah State Licensing Board for Marriage and Family Therapy.

Larson presents workshops nationally and locally on how to predict and enhance marital satisfaction, myths about marriage and mate selection, and marriage preparation and enrichment. He has appeared nationally on *Good Morning America* and the *Today* show and numerous local television and radio stations. Larson has been married to Jeannie Spear Larson for thirty years; they have four children.